LAMBEAU FIELD
GREEN BAY'S NATIONAL TREASURE

*This book would not have been possible without the memorable images
created by the Green Bay Press-Gazette's photographers since 1956,
nor without the careful, precise archiving of thousands of prints, negatives and digital photos
by the Press-Gazette's librarians during that same time.*

"Lambeau Field: Green Bay's National Treasure" stands as a tribute to their talent and to their dedication.

*This book also would not have been possible without the Green Bay Packers' gracious cooperation
in providing Press-Gazette photographers with frequent and extensive access
to the team's facilities at City Stadium and Lambeau Field since 1957.*

Lambeau Field: Green Bay's National Treasure

This book was produced, written and edited by the Green Bay Press-Gazette
with research and editing assistance from the Green Bay Packers.

All photographs are by Green Bay Press-Gazette staff members past and present
with the exception, as noted, of photographs from the Green Bay Packers archive
and the Neville Public Museum of Brown County.

Contents:

Foreword...13

Introduction 14

CHAPTER ONE **The Early Years** 19

CHAPTER TWO **Only at Lambeau** 41

CHAPTER THREE **Unforgettable Games** 53

CHAPTER FOUR **Unforgettable Players**..........77

CHAPTER FIVE **The Stadium Scene** 97

CHAPTER SIX **Game Day** 109

CHAPTER SEVEN **The New Lambeau**.................123

CHAPTER EIGHT **Rededication** 141

◄ The moment for which the Green Bay Packers and their fans have patiently waited for almost three years finally arrives shortly before noon on Sunday, Sept. 7, 2003. Fans in the record crowd of 70,505 rise to their feet, cheering as quarterback Brett Favre runs onto the field during pregame introductions on opening day at Lambeau Field. The $295 million project was completed on time and within budget. The stadium was rededicated at ceremonies at halftime of the game against the Minnesota Vikings.

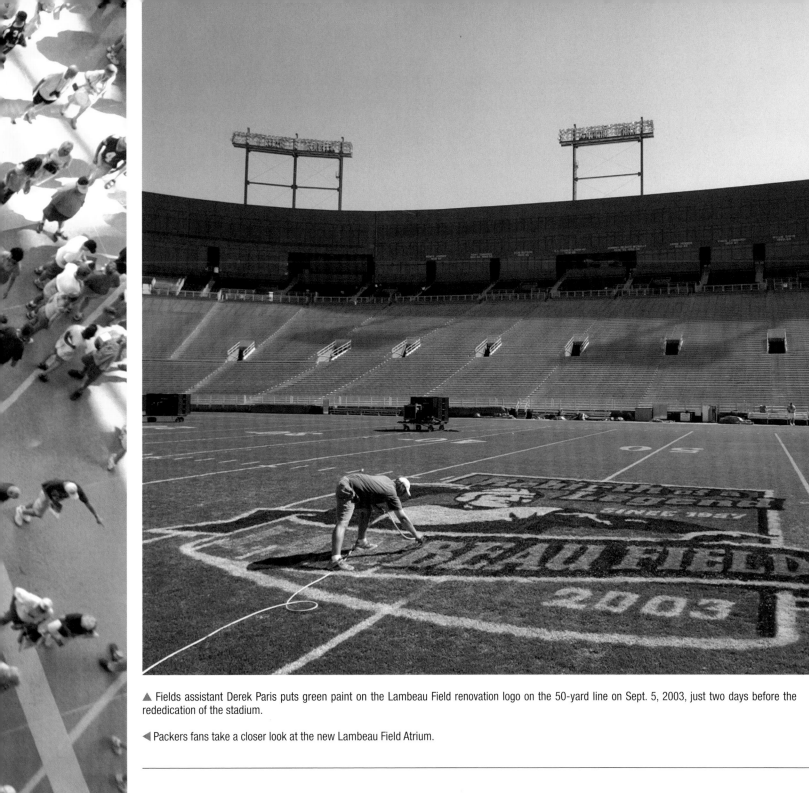

▲ Fields assistant Derek Paris puts green paint on the Lambeau Field renovation logo on the 50-yard line on Sept. 5, 2003, just two days before the rededication of the stadium.

◄ Packers fans take a closer look at the new Lambeau Field Atrium.

▲ The 14-foot bronze statue of legendary Packers coach Vince Lombardi stands watch at Lambeau Field.

◀ Packers fans get their first look at the bronze statues of Curly Lambeau, left, and Vince Lombardi on Aug. 27, 2003. The statues tower over the Robert E. Harlan Plaza outside the entrance to the Lambeau Field Atrium.

▶ Taking advantage of the light at sunrise, Sharon Aspenson of Green Bay takes a photo of her friend, Lois Laverdiere of Ashwaubenon, as she stands at the base of the Curly Lambeau statue on Sept. 5, 2003. They often pass the stadium on their morning walk and decided to get a picture.

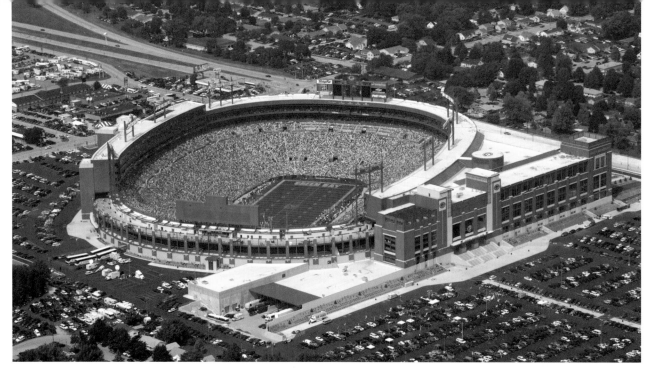

▶ The open south end of Lambeau Field is in the foreground in this photo taken during the season opener against the Minnesota Vikings on Sept. 7, 2003. Neighboring homes in Green Bay are at top.

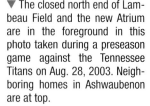

▼ The closed north end of Lambeau Field and the new Atrium are in the foreground in this photo taken during a preseason game against the Tennessee Titans on Aug. 28, 2003. Neighboring homes in Ashwaubenon are at top.

▲ Though more than 11,000 seats were added in the renovation of Lambeau Field, the experience of being in the seating bowl hasn't changed, as people found when they attended the season opener against the Minnesota Vikings on Sept. 7, 2003.

THE IMPORTANCE OF TRADITION

By Bob Harlan
president and chief executive officer
Green Bay Packers

I tend to get very emotional when I talk about Lambeau Field.

This famous address, 1265 Lombardi Ave., has been my office for more than 30 years. And I get the same goose bumps now that I had on June 1, 1971, the first day I drove into the parking lot and started to work in this historic stadium.

Lambeau Field is where Vince Lombardi's championship teams practiced and played, and where Mike Holmgren's Super Bowl winner achieved greatness.

That tradition is very important to me.

In late 1999, when we were trying to decide if we should redevelop Lambeau Field or build a new stadium, fans from across the country called and wrote, begging us to save this stadium.

I found out that our fans love the stadium as much as they love the Packers. And I feel the same way. Lambeau Field is at the core of this franchise's identity.

During the two years of construction, I would drive around the stadium every night after work. I would stop in the parking lot and just stare at this magnificent building. I wanted to check the progress, of course, but I found myself recalling our political battles during the stadium referendum and the important victory we achieved. And

---

◀ Bob Harlan leads a tour of the renovated Lambeau Field on May 14, 2003.

▶ Bob Harlan sits with his wife, Madeline, during the dedication of the Robert E. Harlan Plaza outside the Lambeau Field Atrium on Sept. 2, 2003.

I marveled to think that this fabled stadium sat in the middle of little Green Bay, Wisconsin.

For its combination of beauty, intimacy and ambience, Lambeau Field stands out in a league of its own.

It's the only retro stadium in the National Football League. And I wanted to make sure the Packers' glorious tradition was prominent throughout the building. In the stadium's bowl, we honor Packers who are in the Pro Football Hall of Fame, our world championships and our retired numbers. Our stadium club has rooms named after Johnny Blood, Willie Davis, Paul Hornung and Bart Starr.

The most breathtaking new attraction is at the front of the stadium, where we have 14-foot-high bronze statues of the two most important people in this franchise's proud history — Curly Lambeau and Vince Lombardi.

I always tell people that the Packers' story is more like fiction than reality.

I am so proud of this wonderful book, which traces the history of Lambeau Field, and I am honored to be a part of the most heartwarming story in all of sports.

INTRODUCTION
A TOWN AND ITS STADIUM

Lambeau Field has journeyed through the decades not to reach a destination but to become one. It is a landmark with a legacy. Transcending the form

▲ Packers coach Vince Lombardi, left, and Chicago Bears coach George Halas shake hands after Green Bay's 24-0 victory on Oct. 1, 1961. It was the Packers' first shutout of the Bears since 1935.

and function of a football facility, the venue has acquired mythic stature as a national treasure of professional sports.

Lambeau Field is the physical embodiment of the enduring love affair between a community and its team. From its modest beginning in 1957 to its bold restoration at the dawn of the 21st century, Lambeau Field has evolved into a place that honors time and tradition even as it embraces the expectations of each new season.

Born out of necessity in a pasture on the edge of Green Bay, City Stadium, as it was called for eight years, stood first as a symbol of a community's intense determination to cling to a proud piece of its past.

When the Packers were founded in 1919, Green Bay joined other small cities where the game first took root in the years after World War I. But one by one, other franchises brushed off the dust of small-town America. Only the Packers, a franchise owned then and now by its fans, succeeded in resisting the temptation to move to larger metropolitan venues.

With the 1960s fast approaching, Green Bay, inhabited by 60,000 people, had little in common with the other, bigger host cities in the National Football League. Faced with the likelihood of losing their team because old City Stadium was woefully inadequate, Green Bay residents went to the polls on April 3, 1956, to vote on a $960,000 bond issue to build a 32,150-seat stadium. The measure passed by a 2-1 margin.

Even on Sept. 29, 1957, when the stadium opened to much fanfare, it was one of the few venues in the league built solely and specifically for football. The focal point of every spot "inside the bowl," as the expression goes today, was and still is the green expanse of turf that is just large enough for a football field and sidelines.

Over the years, the stadium and its immediate surroundings developed its own personality. Fans began cooking out in the parking lot before games, ushering in the tradition that came to be known as tailgating. Long a fixture of the local social scene, Packers games became even more popular as seating capacity increased.

It helped, of course, that in 1959, two years after new City Stadium opened, Vince Lombardi came to pace the sidelines in Green Bay. The Packers, who had won just one game in 1958, claimed first place in the NFL's Western Division in 1960.

The Lombardi-era teams' hard-nosed, no-nonsense, gritty style of football meshed perfectly with the sensibilities of the Green Bay area. Most fans were industrious, working-class folks who related to Lombardi's straightforward approach to football almost as a metaphor of life. When Lombardi's second season as general manager and head coach began in 1960, every seat in the stadium was sold for every game. Thus was born the waiting list for season tickets that is the oldest in the NFL.

Green Bay was no stranger to national football prominence. Under the leadership of Earl "Curly" Lambeau, the Packers won six league championships between 1929 and 1944.

But the "Glory Years" ushered in by Lombardi and his players coincided with the full-fledged emergence of football as

a televised sport watched nationwide.

When the Packers played in Green Bay, hundreds of thousands of rabbit-eared black-and-white TVs in the visiting team's NFL city picked up the images of Bart Starr, Jim Taylor, Paul Hornung, Ray Nitschke, Herb Adderley, Willie Davis, Forrest Gregg, Henry Jordan and Willie Wood, as well as views of the stadium where they roamed.

The attraction transcended football. During the 1960s, a time of tumult and transition in the nation, the Green Bay Packers under Lombardi became a soothing counterweight to the cultural revolution that was taking place.

By Sept. 11, 1965, when City Stadium was officially renamed Lambeau Field, the Green Bay Packers and their uncompromising coach were firmly established as a social lifeline to simpler times in a rapidly changing world. Lambeau Field mirrored the image of the team and the city: a place reveling in unapologetic devotion to tradition and timelessness.

Although the Packers won four NFL championships

◄ Tight end Ron Kramer drags Giants linebacker Sam Huff (70) into the end zone and leaves defensive back Joe Morrison (40) in his wake on a 14-yard touchdown pass from Bart Starr in the second quarter of the NFL championship game on Dec. 31, 1961. It was the first of Kramer's two touchdown catches in the game. Giants defensive back Dick Lynch (22) closes in, while Packers end Max McGee (85) walks away.

from 1961 to 1966, the defining moment of the decade for the team and stadium came on Dec. 31, 1967. The temperature was 13 below zero, with a minus-46 wind chill, as the Packers hosted the Dallas Cowboys in a game that will forever be known as the Ice Bowl.

With 13 seconds left to play and without any timeouts, the Packers passed up a game-tying field goal to let quarterback Bart Starr push his way across the goal line for the game-winning touchdown, which gave Green Bay its 5th NFL title under Lombardi and sent it to its second Super Bowl. That game, more than any other moment in its storied history, made Lambeau Field a national icon.

The post-Lombardi era brought little success on the field. But fans still flocked to Lambeau Field. The season-ticket waiting list kept growing, even as bowl seating was expanded and club seats and luxury boxes added.

Happy days returned to Lambeau Field during the 1990s, when the Packers hired Ron Wolf as general manager and Mike Holmgren as coach, then picked up a

▼ Running back Edgar Bennett (34) dives into the end zone on a 1-yard touchdown run during the second quarter of the Packers' 30-27 victory over the Denver Broncos on Oct. 10, 1993.

▲ The pass from quarterback Bart Starr (15) to tight end Marv Fleming (81) comes out of the sky during a 27-10 victory over San Francisco on Oct. 10, 1965. Fleming is covered by 49ers linebacker Dave Wilcox.

young, relatively unknown quarterback from the Atlanta Falcons named Brett Favre. Next came the signing of free-agent defensive end Reggie White.

On their home field, the Packers began to stir the sleeping ghosts of the Lombardi era. As the scent of victory mingled with the aroma of charcoal fires and grilled brats at Lambeau Field, players and fans could hardly contain their enthusiasm. On Dec. 26, 1993, the Lambeau Leap was born after safety LeRoy Butler scored a touchdown on a lateral and jumped over the railing in the south end zone and into the arms of awaiting fans.

The crowning moment of the 1990s came on Jan. 12, 1997. On another bitterly cold winter day at Lambeau Field, the Packers won their first trip to the Super Bowl in 29 years by defeating the Carolina Panthers 30-13. Despite a wind chill of minus-17, the crowd remained in the stands for more than 30 minutes after the game to cheer their team.

Two weeks later, in New Orleans, the Packers defeated the New England Patriots 35-21 to win Super Bowl XXXI. Meanwhile, back in Wisconsin, fans across the state descended on the Lambeau Field parking lot for a spontaneous celebration.

As glorious as the on-the-field successes were for fans, the team found itself facing a long-term financial slide if it could not find new ways to generate revenue. The structure of economics in the NFL, where teams share ticket and television revenue, limited the Packers' access to cash. Without the ability to turn to a deep-pockets owner, the fan-owned Packers had to devise new ways to generate capital.

For most teams in the NFL, that has meant building new stadiums — and at the same time taking a wrecking ball to their history.

"Every place in this league where history has been made has been torn down and replaced," Packers President Bob Harlan said. "Where the great Pittsburgh teams of the '70s played is now a parking lot."

Packers executives, troubled about the team's financial future, considered building new and abandoning Lambeau Field. But the fans, in phone calls, letters and e-mails, said no.

"They said, 'Whatever you do, please save Lambeau Field. Don't build new,'" Harlan said.

So in January 2000, Harlan unveiled a renovation plan to protect the team while preserving the site where the Lombardi teams first etched Lambeau Field into the nation's conscience.

By attaching a massive atrium to the old stadium, the Packers would have a facility that could generate revenue 365 days a year instead of on just 10 game days. But most aspects of the hallowed ground inside the bowl, from the bleacher seats to the natural grass, would not change.

The following September, fans again came to the rescue of their team. Brown County voters approved a 0.5 percent sales tax to provide the biggest slice of funding for the $295 million renovation project, and ticket holders paid a seat license fee.

Completed in time for the start of the 2003 season, the project added a year-round, commercial dimension to Lambeau Field without disturbing its essence: the all-about-football focal point inside the bowl.

As fans from around the nation journey to Green Bay, they marvel at the game-day atmosphere of Lambeau Field, similar to that experienced at college stadiums.

On the occasion of the 40th anniversary of Lambeau Field, in 1997, Philip J. Lowry, author of "Total Football: The Official Encyclopedia of the NFL," told the Green Bay Press-Gazette that there's no place quite like the home of the Packers.

"In football, Lambeau Field is the shrine that Fenway Park and Wrigley Field are to baseball," he said.

"You can feel the soul of the game better at Lambeau Field than anywhere else. There is no other place where you can feel the intensity and the love affair between the city and the team."

▼ Flanked by cheerleaders, the Packers run onto the field before the season opener against the Detroit Lions on Sept. 20, 1970. From left are guard Gale Gillingham (68), tackle Francis Peay (71), center Ken Bowman (57), running back Larry Krause (30) and tackle Bill Hayhoe (77).

CHAPTER ONE

THE EARLY YEARS

Lambeau Field has an aura all its own. To understand what's so special about the stadium, it helps to understand what's so special about the Green Bay Packers.

First, the Packers are the only team in professional sports that is a publicly-owned, nonprofit corporation. The team has 111,507 stockholders — none of whom receives any dividend on his or her initial investment.

The Packers were founded in 1919 when local football star Curly Lambeau and Green Bay Press-Gazette sports editor George W. Calhoun convened two meetings at the newspaper office to form a new city team.

From the beginning, the team's fans have kept the franchise alive. In the earliest years, a hat was passed during games to help defray expenses. Four times in the 20th century, fans came to the financial rescue of the team by purchasing stock: in 1923, 1935, 1950 and 1997.

In the first three sales, fans from the Green Bay area bought most of the stock. In 1997, however, stock was sold to fans from every state and some foreign countries. Fans made their purchases knowing full well they essentially were making a donation.

The Packers have survived and flourished while playing in the smallest city to host a major professional sports franchise.

With a population of just more than 100,000, Green Bay has grown steadily over the years. Yet, during Packers games, home or away, it has the feel of a college town of yesteryear, its streets virtually deserted.

◀ Carl Farah, left, presents a check for $170 to Green Bay Mayor Otto Rachals for the new City Stadium fund. The money was raised from a one-day sale of Pabst Blue Ribbon beer. Farah's new east-side liquor store sold 17,000 bottles or cans of Pabst on July 26, 1957, and donated a penny per bottle or can.

◀ The Packer Lumberjack Band prepares to play at a rally for the new City Stadium at the Columbus Club on March 31, 1956. Packers great Tony Canadeo was the master of ceremonies, and Chicago Bears coach George Halas was a guest speaker. Three days later, on April 3, Green Bay voters overwhelmingly approved construction of a new stadium.

BUILDING NEW CITY STADIUM

By the time the 1950s arrived, Green Bay's professional football facility was more of a liability than a legacy. Complaining that old City Stadium didn't meet modern standards, some NFL owners worked behind the scenes to banish the Packers from the league.

Old City Stadium, behind Green Bay East High School, had inadequate locker room facilities and no toilets. In a league with big-time aspirations, the old stadium had small time written all over it.

The Packers knew it. The city of Green Bay knew it. So did most citizens.

In 1955, a plan was hatched for the people of Green Bay to again come to the Packers' rescue. The city would float a $960,000 bond to build a new stadium. The Packers promised to pay half of the $960,000, which was a key selling point for voters who would have to approve the bond.

For weeks before the referendum on April 3, 1956, proponents of the plan held public meetings to sell the idea. There was even a live television broadcast to discuss the referendum. On Election Day, Green Bay voters enthusiastically approved the project 11,575 to 4,893, a margin of 2 to 1.

Getting the referendum passed proved easier than choosing a new site for the stadium. There were proposals to renovate old City Stadium on the east side and to build in Perkins Park on the west side. The Packers hired a consultant, who suggested farmland in the neighboring town of Ashwaubenon.

In summer 1956, the Packers and the city went west, purchasing 48 acres of farmland from Victor and Florence Vannieuwenhoven for $73,305 and annexing it to the city.

By the end of the year, the city approved plans for the new stadium submitted by John Somerville, a local architect. Geo. M. Hougard & Sons was hired as the general contractor.

Despite sometimes uncooperative weather and brief strikes by carpenters and plumbers, new City Stadium was ready for use for the 1957 season opener against the Chicago Bears on Sept. 29.

Perhaps more important for the future: The design of the new stadium allowed for gradual expansion.

"The stadium contract originally called for a 32,000 seating capacity," Somerville said. "But when we did the geometry, we figured in for 56,000-plus."

That vision — to design and build a stadium that could accommodate gradual expansion — made it possible for the Lambeau Field renovation project to expand seating capacity to 72,515 for the 2003 season.

While the outside of Lambeau Field has been altered dramatically, one thing has not changed: The playing field is in the same place it was on the day the turf was first put down in 1957.

▼ With a hatchet holding down the blueprints, W.C. Green, left, and Louis Conard, both Green Bay Street Department engineers, begin surveying the site of the new City Stadium on Oct. 11, 1956. The tall stake in front of Green marks the location of the future 50-yard line.

◄ City workers using graders begin shaping the east side of the bowl for the new City Stadium in early November 1956. This photo looks north toward Highland Avenue, now Lombardi Avenue. The west side of the stadium was built into the hillside along Ridge Road.

> " I think it has evolved into the best stadium in pro football. Notre Dame Stadium has been voted the best stadium in college football, and Lambeau Field has been voted the best stadium in pro football, and I was fortunate to play in both. There's nothing in the National Football League like Lambeau. When they first built it, it had 32,000 seats, which wasn't much, and they did it on a shoestring. But they've tweaked it through the years to where it's become a hell of a spot, the best stadium in America."
>
> — *Paul Hornung, Packers halfback, 1957-62, 64-66*

▲ The undeveloped site of new City Stadium. *Photo from Green Bay Packers archive*

▲ Architects envisioned this design for the Packers' new stadium in 1956. The four-section design gave way to a natural bowl.

▲ The framework of the press, radio and television box sits atop the west side of the new City Stadium in mid-August 1957. Also new is the low fencing along the seats closest to the field.

▶ Ruth Mann examines a model of the proposed stadium in the lobby of the Brown County Courthouse on Sept. 18, 1956.

▶ The first 400-seat section of concrete steps, on which raised wooden bleacher seats would be installed, is completed at the new City Stadium in April 1957. The 64-foot form is rolled on for pouring the next 400-seat section.

▲ The first steel beams go up on the west side on May 13, 1957. The steel framework held 35 rows of seats above ground level.

▲ These 18 steel-reinforced cement structures, seen in early April 1957, are the main supports for the center portion of the 60-row seating section on the west side.

◀ Harold Baker, a Green Bay Street Department worker, cuts barbed wire from a pasture fence as site work begins for the Packers' new stadium on Oct. 11, 1956. New City Stadium went up on 48 acres of farmland at Highland Avenue, now Lombardi Avenue, and Ridge Road, on what was then the southwest edge of town.

▲ Standing near the south end zone, quarterback Bart Starr looks over progress on construction of new City Stadium in May 1957. A decade later, Starr scored a touchdown not far from where he's standing to give the Packers a 21-17 victory over the Dallas Cowboys in the NFL championship game, better known as the Ice Bowl.

▲ The new scoreboard stands at the back of the south end zone in September 1957. The letter "T" in the word "it" lit up each time the Packers scored a touchdown. When a new scoreboard was erected in the 1960s, the letter "T" in the word "Pabst" did so.

▲ Ronald Haworth operates a ditch digger during the installation of a water-main extension to the new City Stadium on Aug. 14, 1957. He was one of several unlicensed plumbers whose hiring by the city Water Commission prompted a one-day strike by union plumbers.

◄ Martin Mathew holds a sign warning workers to stay off the newly seeded area around the sodded playing field in mid-July 1957. He's standing about where the goal posts would be placed in the south end zone.

◀ The seating area on the west side continues to take shape on May 20, 1957. Crews poured concrete each day to form 400-seat sections of steps, on which raised wooden bleachers would be installed. The steel framework above would hold 35 more rows of seats.

▶ With the new City Stadium behind him, Peter Binsfeld, a member of Plumbers Local 298, walks the picket line at the Highland Avenue entrance to the construction site on Aug. 14, 1957. Work stopped for a day after unlicensed plumbers were hired to install a water-main extension to the stadium.

▲ From left, Clarence Swamp, Andrew Vollmer and Julius Danforth lay sod on the playing field in late June 1957. Above them, a section of seats has been installed to allow workers access to construction on the press box on the west side of the stadium.

◀ Three youngsters — from left, Jeff and Mark Vanden Heuvel and Mike Charles — sit on the seat brackets and watch work in late June 1957. California hardwood planks later were fastened to the brackets.

The Packers' Stadiums

City Stadium/Lambeau Field
Used from 1957 to present.
Renamed Lambeau Field in 1965.

Hagemeister Park
Used from 1919 to 1922. Where
Green Bay East High School is located.
Photo courtesy of the Neville Public Museum of Brown County

City Stadium
Used from 1925 to 1956.
Behind Green Bay East High School.

Bellevue Park
Used from 1923 to 1924. Off of Main Street
just beyond the 1923 Green Bay city limits.
Photo courtesy of the Neville Public Museum of Brown County

The past remembered
A fence, wrought-iron gates and a
sign commemorate the old City
Stadium site at North Baird and East
Walnut streets on Green Bay's east
side. It's still used as the football
field for Green Bay East High School.

Goodbye to old City Stadium, hello to a new one

Football-related hoopla has been at the heart of Green Bay's civic and social infrastructure since the mid-1920s.

So, in 1957, when it came time to have a housewarming for the new stadium it built, Green Bay responded with characteristic exuberance, throwing a weekend-long party.

Even by lofty Green Bay standards, the celebration swelled to epic proportions.

"Green Bay has produced a lot of 'spectaculars' in its long history, but never anything like this," the Green Bay Press-Gazette beamed in a front-page story on Monday, Sept. 30.

Festivities began on Saturday, Sept. 28, the day before the Packers took on the Chicago Bears at the new City Stadium.

A parade through downtown to the site of old City Stadium, behind East High School, attracted 70,000 to 80,000 people, reportedly "the greatest crowd ever" to see a parade in Green Bay.

Once the parade reached old City Stadium, an estimated 18,000 people were in the bleachers, "about two-thirds children who were more interested in Matt Dillon than football nostalgia," the Press-Gazette reported.

James Arness, who played Marshal Matt Dillon in the TV series "Gunsmoke," and Marilyn Van Derbur, who had recently been crowned Miss America, were the featured dignitaries at the farewell ceremony for the east-side City Stadium, home to the Packers for 32 years.

On Saturday evening, an estimated 15,000 people attended a "Venetian Nights" boat show and fireworks display on the Fox River.

The highlight of the weekend came on Sunday. Sunny skies and mild temperatures greeted the 32,132 fans who attended the first game at the new 32,150-seat City Stadium on Green Bay's far southwest side.

The halftime ceremony featured remarks by Vice President Richard Nixon and at least eight other politicians and NFL officials, all of whom lavished praise on the city and new stadium.

To cap off the weekend, the Packers upset the Bears, who were favored by a touchdown. Babe Parilli threw a 6-yard, fourth-quarter touchdown pass to Gary Knafelc to help the Packers to a 21-17 victory.

Green Bay's opening-day triumph sent the crowd home happy, but not quickly.

Officials expressed concern that it took 40 minutes to clear the 6,500-space parking lot.

Still, the weekend was touted as an overwhelming success.

The next day, an item in the Press-Gazette read, "Anyone who wasn't satisfied is the kind of fellow who would growl about not getting eggs in his beer."

▲ Standing in foreground, Vice President Richard Nixon speaks to the crowd during halftime ceremonies at the first game at new City Stadium, Sept. 29, 1957. Dignitaries and team officials sit on the stage behind him. The Packers' cheerleaders stand on the field behind them.

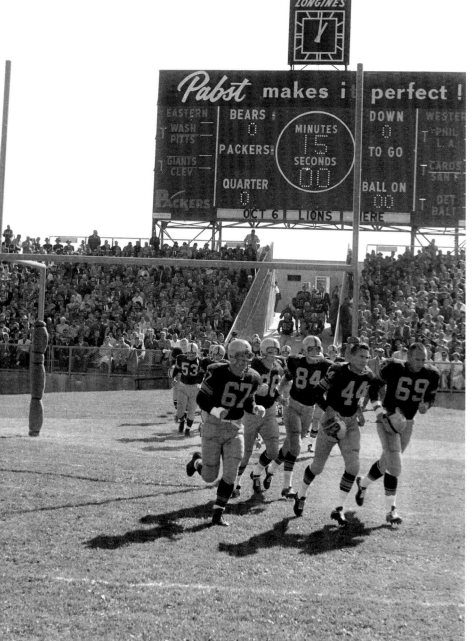

◄ This banner celebrated the opening of new City Stadium.

▼ From left, U.S. Rep. John Byrnes, Wisconsin Gov. Vernon Thomson, Miss America Marilyn Van Derbur, Vice President Richard Nixon and former Green Bay Mayor Dominic Olejniczak, a member of the Packers' board of directors, are among the dignitaries at the Packers' first game at new City Stadium.

▲ The Packers run onto the field before the first game at the new City Stadium. From left are defensive back Sam Palumbo (53), guard Jim Salsbury (67), end Billy Howton (86), end Gary Knafelc (84), defensive back Bobby Dillon (44) and linebacker Bill Forester (69).

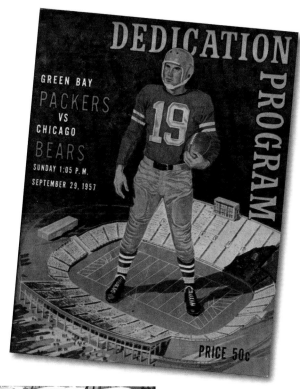

▲ From left, Mr. and Mrs. Glenn Hudson and Mr. and Mrs. M.W. Sherman take in the Packers' first game.

▶ Cars fill the parking lot at the Packers' first game.

▲ Program from new City Stadium dedication ceremonies and Packers-Bears game, Sept. 29, 1957.

> ❝ I'd have to say the best day for me was the Dedication Day, the first game in that stadium against the Bears. I caught the winning touchdown pass so that will always be special to me. Having played in the old stadium and moving to the new one was quite a change. They haven't messed with the integrity of the stadium; they still have the original bowl. All of the great games that have been played there and all of the great players that have run out onto that field makes it very special.❞
>
> — *Gary Knafelc, Packers end, 1954-62*

NAMING IT AFTER LAMBEAU

In an age when stadium names owe more to corporate marketing schemes than legend, lore or place, Lambeau Field stands alone as a monument to athletic accomplishment.

The only professional football stadium to bear the name of a former NFL player, Green Bay's City Stadium was rededicated to honor Earl Louis "Curly" Lambeau on Sept. 11, 1965.

Lambeau died of a heart attack in Sturgeon Bay on June 1, 1965. He was 67. Friends said he was mowing the lawn at the time.

Lambeau was just 21 when he founded the Green Bay Packers in 1919 with the help of the Indian Packing Co. and George W. Calhoun, the sports editor of the Green Bay Press-Gazette.

Lambeau has been described as "an incurable optimist ... a man of vast energy, invincible confidence and mesmeric charm." His teams compiled a 212-106-21 record in NFL games in his 31 years as coach of the Packers.

Lambeau is regarded as a "pioneer of the forward pass" because he installed it as a regular offensive weapon in the 1920s, an era when many coaches and fans disparaged advancing the ball by air.

Though he cut formal ties with the Packers in 1950

◄ Packers founder Curly Lambeau, left, wearing glasses and dark suit, arrives for the team's game against the Chicago Bears on Sept. 27, 1959. It was Vince Lombardi's first regular-season game as coach.

under less-than-amicable circumstances, Lambeau's emotional bond with the team remained intact.

He said so in 1960, while at his Palm Springs, Calif., winter home:

"When the Packers came out there back in 1956 and 1957, the newspapers would say, 'The lowly Packers are coming to town' — and it hurt. Your heart tells you who you are for," he is quoted as saying in the 1961 edition of the Green Bay Packers Yearbook.

Though some around Green Bay criticized Lambeau for his flamboyant, fast-living lifestyle, others moved quickly after his death to honor his memory.

The first time the words "Lambeau Field" appeared in public was on June 10, 1965.

That day, the Press-Gazette reported that the Greater Green Bay Labor Council had unanimously adopted a resolution "that the name of Green Bay City Stadium be changed to 'Lambeau Stadium' or 'Lambeau Field.'"

The resolution was delivered to city officials, who were reportedly not wild about the idea.

On June 16, the Press-Gazette published an editorial aimed at coaxing city officials out of their reluctance.

"Since his career has been closed by death it seems fitting for the city to honor his memory by giving his name to the field on which the Green Bay Packers will carry on in the future," the newspaper said.

City officials weren't the only ones less than enthusiastic about renaming City Stadium after Lambeau.

Vince Lombardi, then coach and general manager of the Packers, was critical of the idea, said Lee Remmel, the Packers' executive director of public relations. Remmel was on the Press-Gazette staff at the time.

Lombardi was "vehemently opposed to the idea ... and spoke out against it in public a couple of times," Remmel said.

For the record, Lombardi said he believed it was more important for Green Bay, the city, to be promoted by the national media than an individual, Remmel recalled.

"There was speculation that Lombardi was not fond of the idea because he wanted the stadium to be named after him someday," Remmel said. "I never heard him say that, but he did have a substantial ego."

By the beginning of summer, city officials had agreed to change the stadium's name to Lambeau Field.

As Remmel puts it, "that was one game Lombardi lost ... he got the street, Lambeau got the stadium, and I think deservedly so."

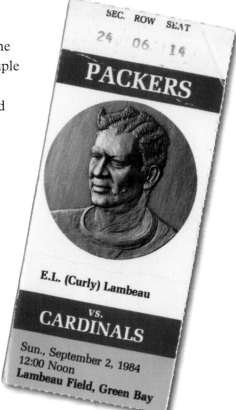

▲ Ticket stub from Packers-Cardinals game, Sept. 2, 1984. When Lambeau left the Packers, he became coach of the Chicago Cardinals.

◄ This plaque, recognizing team founder Curly Lambeau and the Packers' presidents from 1923 to 1957, was placed in City Stadium in November 1960.

THIS PLAQUE ERECTED BY THE GREEN BAY PACKERS IN HONOR OF THE FOLLOWING INDIVIDUALS WHO HAVE CONTRIBUTED GREATLY TO THE SUCCESS OF THE GREEN BAY PACKERS AND HENCE TO THE BUILDING OF THIS STADIUM

EARL W. (CURLY) LAMBEAU
COACH AND GENERAL MANAGER 1919-1949

ANDREW B. TURNBULL
PRESIDENT 1923-27

RAYMOND E. EVRARD
PRESIDENT 1928

Dr. WEBBER W. KELLY
PRESIDENT 1929

LELAND H. JOANNES
PRESIDENT 1930-46

EMIL W. FISCHER
PRESIDENT 1947-52

RUSSELL W. BOGDA
PRESIDENT 1953-57

CONSTRUCTION TIMELINE

From the moment it was conceived, the stadium that would become Lambeau Field was designed to be expanded.

Before the major renovation that began in 2001, the seating capacity inside the stadium had been increased seven times since 1957.

1957: Opened with 32,150 seats.

1961: Added 6,519 seats, to 38,669.

1963: Added 3,658 seats, to 42,327. The Packers also built a new administration building at the stadium, 1265 Highland Ave.

1965: Added 8,525 seats, to 50,852.

1970: Added 5,411 seats, to 56,263.

1985: Seating capacity expanded to 56,926 with the construction of 72 private boxes, the first at Lambeau Field.

1990: The Packers spend $8.263 million to erect 36 new boxes and add 1,920 club seats. Capacity is at 59,543 with the addition of 2,617 seats.

1995: The north end zone is enclosed with 90 more private boxes, which cost the Packers $4.7 million. Seating capacity is 60,890.

2002: The partially completed renovation adds 4,400 seats, bringing capacity to 65,290.

2003: The $295 million renovation is finished, bringing capacity to 72,515.

◄ City Stadium's lights cut through the haze during a preseason game against the New York Giants on Sept. 3, 1962, a wet, steamy late-summer night. *Photo from the Henry Lefebvre Collection of the Neville Public Museum of Brown County*

▼ The light towers on the west side of City Stadium stand tall behind the Packers' new $175,000 administration building in September 1963.

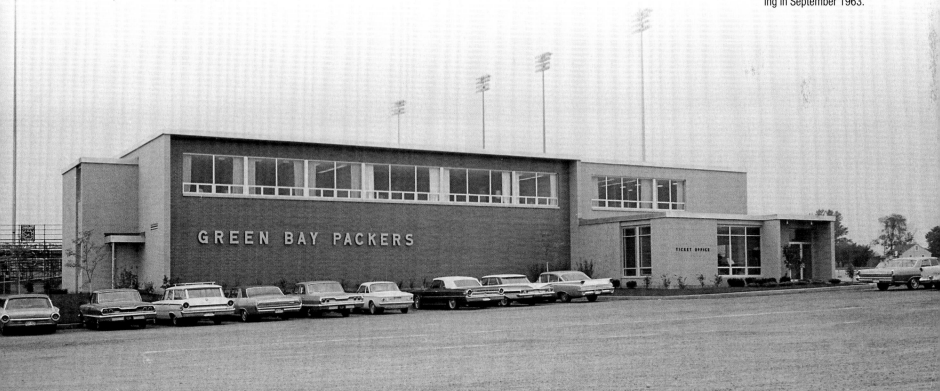

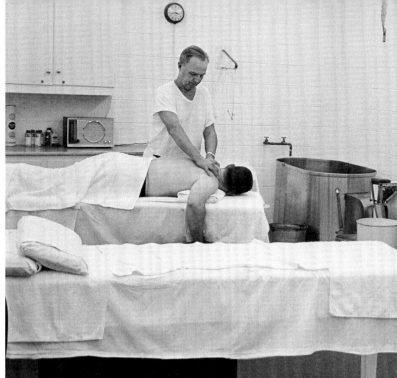

▲ Trainer Bud Jorgensen, left, and equipment manager Dad Braisher pose with equipment in the Packers' new locker room in September 1963. The room featured plush green carpeting.

▲ The City Stadium press box and bleachers are visible out the window of publicist Tom Miller's office in the Packers' new $175,000 administration building in July 1963.

▲ Bud Jorgensen provides treatment in the Packers' new training room, nicknamed the "White Room," in September 1963.

▶ Vince Lombardi and his coaching staff sit in the Packers' new classroom in September 1963. Lombardi is second from left.

▲ Coach and general manager Vince Lombardi sits at his desk in his spacious office in the Packers' new administration building in September 1963.

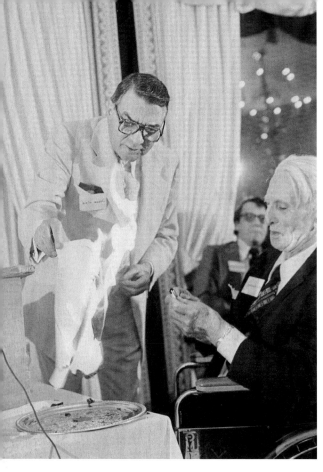

◀ The Packers Pro Shop — identified in this August 1989 photo as the "Packer Pro Gift Shop" — opened that year with a small selection of souvenir items in about 800 square feet of retail space. Today's Packers Pro Shop is about eight times larger, with two floors of display space and a much more extensive inventory.

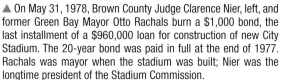

▲ On May 31, 1978, Brown County Judge Clarence Nier, left, and former Green Bay Mayor Otto Rachals burn a $1,000 bond, the last installment of a $960,000 loan for construction of new City Stadium. The 20-year bond was paid in full at the end of 1977. Rachals was mayor when the stadium was built; Nier was the longtime president of the Stadium Commission.

> I've had the privilege of seeing every game played at Lambeau Field since it opened in September of 1957, and I think it's in a class by itself today as a football shrine, for a variety of reasons. Primarily because of its great history — the Packers have won three of their last four NFL championships in Lambeau, including the legendary Ice Bowl.
>
> "Also because of its remarkable intimacy — the fans can almost reach out from the stands and shake hands with the players and heroes. And lastly because of the Lambeau Leap, a unique interaction between player and fans that sets it apart. I can readily see why Lambeau has been voted one of the top 10 sports venues in the world."
>
> — *Lee Remmel, Packers executive director of public relations*

▲ Light towers lie in the east parking lot in February 1985. They were taken down to allow construction of the first luxury boxes at Lambeau Field.

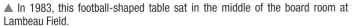

▲ In 1983, this football-shaped table sat in the middle of the board room at Lambeau Field.

▶ The Packers' locker room was remodeled over the summer of 1983, using green-and-gold carpet with the Packers' G. The project also added offices, racquetball courts, a media room and lounges for players and coaches in the Packers' administration building.

▲ Bob Fojut, left, and Dale Schweitzer apply caulking compound to the luxury boxes on the east side of Lambeau Field in mid-July 1985. The photo was taken with a wide-angle lens.

CHAPTER TWO

ONLY AT LAMBEAU

From time to time over the years, the community has come together at Lambeau Field for events other than Packers games.

This was especially true in the earlier years of the stadium's life.

With a seating capacity at one time large enough to more than accommodate the adult population of Green Bay, the stadium has been a venue for a number of special events.

Hundreds of former local high school football players can say they participated in games on the same field as the legendary Green Bay Packers.

In 1963, when the facility was still known as City Stadium, Green Bay's East and West high schools clashed on the same turf as Vince Lombardi's championship team. The game, the 58th renewal of one of the oldest intra-city rivalries in Wisconsin, ended in a 0-0 tie.

Through the late 1960s, the stadium was the home field for two Green Bay high school football teams — the West Wildcats, who started playing there in 1957, and the Southwest Trojans, who debuted there in 1965. The 1956 campaign for the stadium referendum included a promise that the new facility would be used as West's home field. Lombardi eventually halted the practice.

In 1976, as the nation celebrated its bicentennial, comedian Bob Hope made a visit to Green Bay. Despite rainy weather, 18,000 people showed up at Lambeau Field for Hope's appearance over Memorial Day weekend.

In 1985, the rock group Survivor played at Fun Fest in July. The attendance of 13,000 for the concert set a record for the biggest crowd to attend a single musical performance in Green Bay.

The largest crowds to show up at Lambeau Field for something other than a Packers game came for fireworks. ShopKo, a national department store chain with headquarters not far from the stadium, sponsored annual fireworks displays on the Fourth of July. All available seats filled quickly for the fireworks shows, which later were moved to downtown Green Bay.

▲ All-access pass from Survivor concert at Fun Fest at Lambeau Field, July 26-28, 1985.

◄ The crowd fills just a portion of City Stadium during the Green Bay East-Green Bay West high school football game on Nov. 2, 1963. *Photo from the Neville Public Museum of Brown County*

▶ A Green Bay West High School player carries the ball against Green Bay East in their game at City Stadium on Nov. 2, 1963. West is wearing the dark jerseys; East the light jerseys. The 58th annual game between the crosstown rivals ended in a 0-0 tie. *Photo from the Neville Public Museum of Brown County*

▲ Lucia Subano (1) leads a group of runners through Lambeau Field during the first Cellcom Green Bay Marathon on June 25, 2000. The stadium renovation project forced organizers to reroute the marathon past Lambeau Field in each of the next three years.

▶ Actor Robert Preston, at left in front of camera, and longtime Packers fan Howard Blindauer, wearing tie, stand outside the Packers' offices in July 1965, preparing for a take as a TV crew begins filming an hour-long program on Wisconsin.

One of the more unusual non-football uses of Lambeau Field came in 2000, the year before renovation work began. In the first year of the Cellcom Green Bay Marathon, the Packers opened

▲ This is the only time a Packers player has ever worn No. 3 at the stadium, during a 35-17 victory over the Los Angeles Rams on Nov. 19, 1961. Hall of Famer Tony Canadeo's number was retired in 1952, but was issued by mistake nine years later, when kicker Ben Agajanian was signed to fill in while Paul Hornung was in the military.

the gates of the stadium to allow race participants to run through Lambeau Field as the game-day sound track echoed through the stadium.

Other only-at-Lambeau experiences:

• Lambeau Field has been sold out on a season-ticket basis since 1960.

The only NFL teams that even came close to matching the Packers' record were the Washington Redskins and the Denver Broncos, and both of those teams have moved to new stadiums.

▲ Bishop Stanislaus V. Bona, the leader of Northeastern Wisconsin's large Catholic population, throws the ceremonial first pass before the Bishop's Charities preseason game against the New York Giants on Aug. 14, 1965. Coach Vince Lombardi, a devout Catholic, agreed to start the benefit game in 1961. The Packers have hosted the game each year since.

◀ Because Maryland sod put down for the NFC championship game in January 1997 wouldn't grow in Green Bay's climate, the Packers allowed it to be torn up, boxed and sold for charity after the game. Amy Hogan sells a box to Dr. James Jerzak, one of the thousands of fans who snapped up a piece of the Frozen Tundra at $10 a box in January and February of that year.

▼ When Lambeau Field's natural grass field was torn up in early 1997 and replaced with a hybrid surface of natural grass and synthetic turf, some local entrepreneurs bought some of the old dirt and sold it as Packers Paydirt for $9.95 a jar.

With a waiting list of 60,000 names, the Packers are virtually assured of sellouts at Lambeau Field for years to come. The waiting list for seats at Lambeau is one of the longest in the league. Those at the bottom of the Packers' waiting list have an estimated 30-year wait before they will be given the opportunity to buy season tickets.

• Unlike at most professional sports venues, where part-time employees work at concession stands, the person handing you a hot dog is likely a volunteer.

At every game, Lambeau Field hosts hundreds of volunteers from local civic and church groups who work the concession stands inside the stadium.

The charitable organizations earn a portion of the money collected at each concession stand. For many, the money earned during the Packers season represents their largest fund-raiser of the year.

• Packers fans so love Lambeau Field that they'll even pay for its dirt.

One of the most unusual fund-raisers in the history of professional sports took place in the parking lot of Lambeau Field on Jan. 25, 1997.

To raise cash for four local organizations, the Packers allowed pieces of Lambeau Field sod to be sold to the public for $10 a box.

The sod was from the NFC championship game against the Carolina Panthers on Jan. 12, 1997, when the Packers won their first trip to the Super Bowl in 29

▶ Children try their own Lambeau Leaps during the May 19, 2001, bill-signing ceremonies at the stadium.

years.

Response to the sod sale surprised even longtime Green Bay residents. Every piece of sod — 22,000 boxes — sold in two hours. Thousands of fans went without.

On Feb. 22 and 23, a second round of sod sales was held. Proceeds from that sale benefited the Packers, helping pay for new turf that was installed at Lambeau Field before the 1997 season.

• If ever there was a ritual of celebration that reflects the bond between players and fans, it is the Lambeau Leap.

Invented in a moment of sheer delight, on a bitter-cold December day in 1993, the Lambeau Leap has endured through the years as an act of shared exuberance.

The official Lambeau Leap takes place only when a fully padded Packer, having scored a touchdown, hurls himself over the railing into the arms of awaiting fans in one of the end zones.

Usually completed with grace by high-flying wide receivers and defensive backs, the leap has sometimes been executed with less finesse by bulkier running backs and tight ends.

Safety LeRoy Butler was the first to launch himself into the first row of fans for a group hug.

On Dec. 26, 1993, in a game against the Los Angeles Raiders, Butler knocked the ball loose after a swing pass to the Raiders' Randy Jordan. Defensive end Reggie White recovered the ball, ran 10 yards

and lateraled it to Butler, who sprinted 25 yards for a touchdown.

After crossing the goal line, Butler kept going. He threw himself into the stands of the south end zone.

"Those fans were pumped," Butler said after the game. "They were screaming and yelling. It makes you feel good. It makes you play good, too."

While many a fan has been jostled and lots of beer has been spilled, no fans or players have reported injuries as a result of the Lambeau Leap.

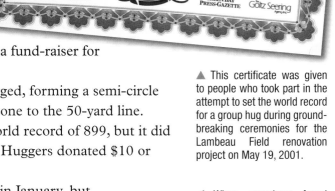

• As part of groundbreaking ceremonies on May 19, 2001, for the $295 million stadium renovation, attendees were invited to participate in a group hug as a fund-raiser for Special Olympics.

All told, 872 people hugged, forming a semi-circle that ran from the south end zone to the 50-yard line. The effort fell short of the world record of 899, but it did raise $30,000 for the charity. Huggers donated $10 or $15 to participate.

Renovation work began in January, but groundbreaking ceremonies were delayed to take advantage of warmer weather.

• At the first Monday night game after the Sept. 11, 2001, terrorist attacks against America, a red-, white- and blue-clad crowd watched as Packers linebacker Chris Gizzi, an Air Force reservist, led the team onto the field

▲ This certificate was given to people who took part in the attempt to set the world record for a group hug during ground-breaking ceremonies for the Lambeau Field renovation project on May 19, 2001.

◄ When organizers found themselves lacking enough people to circle the Lambeau Field stands in a group hug, they closed the circle by drop-ping the line onto the playing field. The attempt at a world record drew 872 people, just 28 short of setting the mark.

while waving the American flag.

Players from the Packers and Washington Redskins joined 150 area police officers and firefighters in holding a 90-by-120-foot flag shaped like the United States.

The audience shared a moment of silence for the attack victims, but also broke out into spontaneous chants of "U.S.A.! U.S.A.! U.S.A.!"

Celestial fireworks greeted the newly renovated Lambeau Field even before its official rededication.

Torrential rains doused players and fans during much of the first half of a preseason game against the Tennessee Titans on Aug. 28, 2003. Then the game was suspended and the stands cleared because of lightning — believed to be a first at Lambeau Field, or at any Packers game in Green Bay.

The wait wasn't short. Play was suspended for 2 hours and 33 minutes, resuming at 11:01 p.m.

An estimated 15,000 to 20,000 faithful fans stayed to see play resume, only to witness an otherwise forgettable 27-3 drubbing that didn't end until 12:46 a.m.

The only quick thing about the night was a nickname: the Lightning Bowl.

▲ Packers linebacker Chris Gizzi, a member of the Air Force Reserve, runs onto the field, carrying the American flag before the Packers' game against the Washington Redskins on Sept. 24, 2001. It was the first Monday night game after the Sept. 11 terrorist attacks.

▲ Fans gather near an entrance to the Lambeau Field seating area as they wait out heavy rain and lightning, which forced a 2½-hour delay in the Packers' preseason game against the Tennessee Titans on Aug. 28, 2003. It was believed to be the first game ever suspended because of bad weather in Green Bay.

◄ Fans gather their belongings as they leave their seats shortly before halftime on Aug. 28, 2003. Heavy rain and lightning forced NFL officials to halt the game and clear the seating area for safety reasons.

▶ Deputy Police Chief Harold Compton, left, shows his badge to Packers center Ken Bowman before arresting him and 19 other Packers and players from the Chicago Bears, Washington Redskins and St. Louis Cardinals on July 25, 1974. Deputy Chief Fred Mathews stands between them. NFL veterans were on strike that summer and were picketing a scrimmage between Packers and Bears rookies and free agents despite a restraining order obtained by the Packers to keep them at a distance from Lambeau Field.

▼ With the Vietnam War being waged half a world away, Packers fans show their patriotism by waving U.S. flags at the end of the national anthem at the Dec. 7, 1968, home finale against the Baltimore Colts. Three Green Bay women — Annabell Dollar, Annette Fuller and Janet Santaga — organized the tribute, and local merchants raised $6,000 to buy the flags. Harry Hulmes, the Colts' general manager, said: "I seriously doubt if this sort of thing could be held any place in the country except Green Bay."

▲ Apparently released near the south end zone, a pheasant runs on the field at the end of the first quarter of a game against the St. Louis Cardinals on Nov. 11, 1973. To the delight of the crowd, the bird went 99 yards before stepping out of bounds on the 1-yard line, then wandered back onto the field and into the end zone. An official grabbed the pheasant and gave it to Jack Noel, the manager of the visitors' locker room. Noel put the bird in a box and took it to the Packers' locker room. The next day, the pheasant was taken to the Bay Beach Wildlife Sanctuary.

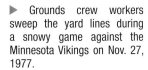

▶ Grounds crew workers sweep the yard lines during a snowy game against the Minnesota Vikings on Nov. 27, 1977.

▼ Green Bay residents cheer for the Packers in a mock snowstorm staged at Lambeau Field in February 1986 for an Alka-Seltzer Plus commercial. A New York advertising agency tried to re-create the Snow Bowl, played the previous Dec. 1, for the spot.

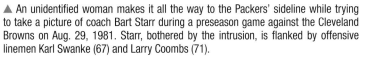

▲ An unidentified woman makes it all the way to the Packers' sideline while trying to take a picture of coach Bart Starr during a preseason game against the Cleveland Browns on Aug. 29, 1981. Starr, bothered by the intrusion, is flanked by offensive linemen Karl Swanke (67) and Larry Coombs (71).

▲ Assistant coach Zeke Bratkowski gives President Gerald Ford a tour of the Packers' weight room on April 3, 1976. Defensive tackle Mike McCoy (76) continues his workout during the tour. Ford, who played college football at Michigan, was in Green Bay for dedication of the Packer Hall of Fame.

◀ Fans parade around the field after tearing down the goal posts in the south end zone after the Packers' 22-13 victory over the Atlanta Falcons in the 1975 season finale on Dec. 21. Doing so was a little curious. The Packers finished 4-10, but had rallied after losing eight of their first nine games to start the season.

▲ Packers nose tackle Jerry Boyarsky, left, and center Mark Cannon walk the picket line at the Lombardi Avenue entrance to the Lambeau Field parking lot on Sept. 29, 1987. Cannon was the team's player representative to the union, which went on strike in search of better benefits and free agency.

◀ Packers fans send a message to striking players during a 19-16 loss to the Detroit Lions in a game using replacement players on Oct. 11, 1987. The Packers were 0-1-1 when the strike started in late September, and the replacement players won two of the three games they played before the regulars returned a month later.

◀ Defensive back Chuck Washington (38) and receiver Cornelius Redick (87) acknowledge the fans' cheers after the Packers' 16-10 overtime victory over the Philadelphia Eagles in a replacement game on Oct. 18, 1987. The regular players returned the next week.

▲ Packers players walk through a crowd estimated at 7,000 fans at Fan Photo Day in the Lambeau Field parking lot on Aug. 1, 1982. The player wearing No. 66 near the bottom of the photo is offensive lineman Larry Pfohl. He never made the Packers, but became famous as professional wrestler Lex Luger. The Packers didn't retire Hall of Fame linebacker Ray Nitschke's No. 66 until 1983. Only two players — linebacker Paul Rudzinski in 1978 and nose tackle Mike Lewis in 1980 — wore No. 66 during the regular season after Nitschke retired in 1972.

▲ Jerry Kramer (64), Ken Bowman (57) and Fuzzy Thurston (63) help teammate Bart Starr (15) re-enact his Ice Bowl-winning touchdown sneak in the south end zone during a fantasy camp at Lambeau Field on June 14, 1992.

▶ Defensive tackle Esera Tuaolo sings the national anthem before the Packers' game against the Chicago Bears on Oct. 17, 1991.

▲ Bubba Depew, a program manager at a Green Bay radio station, is one of 30 people to do the wave — from each seat in the stadium, one seat at a time — to raise money for charity on June 11, 1996. It took six hours. Another radio personality, Steve Davis, took four days to do so alone in 1995.

▶ Thanksgiving was still a couple of weeks away when this turkey wandered onto the field, causing a two-minute delay at the start of the second quarter of the Packers' 20-13 loss to the Indianapolis Colts on Nov. 13, 1988. The bird was apparently smuggled into the stadium. A Brown County Sheriff's Department officer carried it from the field.

▲ Don Berg is part of the crowd of 18,707 at the Packers' first shareholders meeting at Lambeau Field on July 8, 1998.

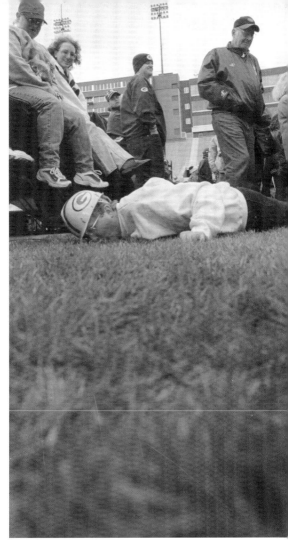

▲ Frank Lamping of Union Grove kisses the Lambeau Field turf "at least three times, as of last count" to show his love of the Packers. He did so, realizing a lifelong dream, on May 19, 2001, during ceremonies at which Wisconsin Gov. Tommy Thompson signed a bill authorizing a referendum on the proposed renovation of Lambeau Field.

◀ Not knowing how many people would attend the annual shareholders meeting after gaining almost 106,000 new shareholders in the stock sale of 1997 and 1998, the Packers moved the 1998 meeting to Lambeau Field.

CHAPTER THREE

UNFORGETTABLE GAMES

Just going to Lambeau Field can be memorable. But over the course of more than four decades, some games stand out. Fixed in the hearts and minds of Packers fans everywhere, these unforgettable games have become legendary.

From 1957 to 2002, before Lambeau Field's latest renovation, it hosted 238 regular-season and postseason games. Here are the top 20.

DEC. 31, 1967
THE ICE BOWL
PACKERS 21, COWBOYS 17

If any one game thrust Green Bay and its football stadium into the national consciousness, it was the Ice Bowl, perhaps the only NFL game to have its own enduring nickname.

With 13 seconds to play and without any timeouts, the Packers pass up a game-tying field goal and win the NFL title with a Bart Starr touchdown sneak. The temperature is 13 below,

with a minus-46 wind chill. It's the coldest professional football game ever played, as long as records have been kept, and will forever be known as the Ice Bowl. Starr follows the blocks of guard Jerry Kramer and center Ken Bowman, a play regarded as one of the most recognizable in the history of football. The game, voted the greatest ever by many media outlets, gives the Packers an unprecedented third consecutive NFL championship. The win sends the Packers to their second Super Bowl and is the last game coached at Lambeau Field by the legendary Vince Lombardi.

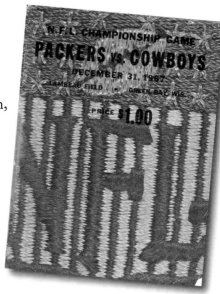

◀ The referees signal touchdown as Bart Starr (15) dives across the goal line for the game-winning score.

▶ Coach Vince Lombardi watches from the sidelines.

> " There have been and continue to be special moments in that stadium. In my own mind it comes down to the Ice Bowl. One, because of the significance of that game, the fact that we were going for our third consecutive championship. Two, combine that with the weather and you really had something special. I don't know how our wives sat there, but they did."
>
> — *Bart Starr, Packers quarterback, 1956-71, head coach, 1975-83*

Dec. 31, 1967
The Ice Bowl
Packers 21, Cowboys 17

*This account was written by
Green Bay Press-Gazette columnist Warren Gerds,
who was on the sidelines that day.*

You're on the field during the Ice Bowl.

The cold is like a wrench twisting every joint. You fear for your eyes. Breathing is like sniffing little daggers.

Near the Dallas Cowboys bench, an Associated Press photographer squints against the low sun of Dec. 31, 1967.

He pulls the metal camera from his face. White. His nose is frostbitten. He puts the camera up for another shot.

At minus 13 degrees, flesh freezes on contact with metal.

For a championship game, Lambeau Field is strangely quiet. Early scores by the Green Bay Packers produce muffled enthusiasm from the sellout crowd of 50,861. Gloves and bundling soak up sound.

The Cowboys move like robots. They speak little. Their emotions seem frozen.

One of their prize targets — receiver "Bullet" Bob Hayes, the "world's fastest human" from the Olympics — runs patterns with his hands tucked in his pants.

Only one thing melts — Green Bay's 14-0 lead.

Packers quarterback Bart Starr fumbles when hit. Dallas scores.

Near halftime — thunk! — Dallas

▲ Cornerback Herb Adderley (26) intercepts a Don Meredith pass in the second quarter. Linebacker Dave Robinson (89) is at left.

▲ With tackle Forrest Gregg (75) and guard Jerry Kramer (64) leading the way, quarterback Bart Starr dives across the goal line for the game-winning touchdown. Kramer and center Ken Bowman keep Cowboys defensive tackle Jethro Pugh (75) out of the play.

kicker Danny Villanueva whacks a field goal in a major effort from 21 yards.

Halftime spells little relief for fans. No entertainment. No heat. A wind chill of 46 below.

At home, fans listen on WBAY radio. There is no CBS-TV broadcast in Green Bay or Wausau because of a blackout rule.

To start the fourth quarter, Dallas halfback Dan Reeves arches a surprise 50-yard touchdown pass to end Lance Rentzel. Cowboys 17, Packers 14.

Sunlight grows dim. Long shadows make the field's dead-brown grass feel colder.

A realization creeps in: This may be the end.

The Packers struggle. The Cowboys continue their quiet, mechanical ways.

With 4:50 left, the Packers get the ball at their 32.

The ground is like concrete. Fingers are icy. The ball is like a

▲ A saxophone player in the Packer Band is dressed for the weather.

doorstop.

Starr throws wobblers. They're caught.

Starr is sacked. Packers end Boyd Dowler leaves after his head is bounced on the ground.

The Packers get a break: Castoff fullback Chuck Mercein gathers in a screen pass and charges to the Dallas 11.

The conclusive setup: No Packers timeouts, the ball at the Cowboys' 1, 17 seconds left — score or lose.

Starr sneaks, Packers celebrate.

It's not over. Thirteen seconds are left. But Dallas passes fail.

At 0:00, fans swarm over railings and rush the goal posts. Mob power takes over the field.

Everybody there knows they and the Packers endured a classic trial.

▲ Linebacker Lee Roy Caffey (60) flattens Cowboys running back Craig Baynham for a 3-yard loss on a pass from Don Meredith in the fourth quarter.

▶ From left, quarterback Zeke Bratkowski, cornerback Doug Hart, tackle Forrest Gregg, running back Donny Anderson, safety Tom Brown and linebacker Tommy Joe Crutcher celebrate in the Packers' locker room.

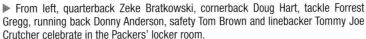

▲ A wistful-looking Vince Lombardi, his hat taken from his head by a fan after the game, is escorted from the field by Willard Jackson, the director of the stadium workers. It was Lombardi's last game as Packers coach at Lambeau Field.

▲ Quarterback Bart Starr, his face swollen from the cold, talks to reporters at his locker after the game.

▶ A cigarette dangling from his mouth, Cowboys quarterback Don Meredith talks to reporters after the game. "It wasn't a fair test of football," he said. "That cold hurt both teams."

▲ Undeterred by the cold, Packers fans tear down the goal posts after the game.

◀ Oscar Mellenthin of Beaver Dam makes some soup to try to stay warm.

SEPT. 29, 1957
HOME SWEET HOME
PACKERS 21, BEARS 17

On Green Bay's southwest side, the new City Stadium is dedicated with great fanfare. Vice President Richard Nixon, Miss America Marilyn Van Derbur and TV star James Arness — Marshal Matt Dillon on "Gunsmoke" — show up for the festivities. The day is made even sweeter for Packers fans when quarterback Babe Parilli hits Gary Knafelc with the winning touchdown pass in the fourth quarter.

▲ Billy Howton (86) scores the Packers' first touchdown at new City Stadium, catching a 37-yard pass from Babe Parilli and outrunning the Bears' Ray Gene Smith (20). It tied the game at 7 early in the second quarter.

▲ Gary Knafelc, on ground behind goal post, scores the game-winning touchdown. Ron Kramer (88) celebrates at left and Billy Howton (86) is at right.

▶ Bobby Dillon intercepts a pass, taking it away from the Bears' Harlon Hill, to end Chicago's last threat late in the fourth quarter. John Petitbon (20) and the Bears' Gene Schroeder (88) close in on the play.

▲ Fans in the south end zone stands cheer as the Packers' defense stops the Bears' final drive.

◄ Linebacker Bill Forester (71) gets past Bears tackle John Mellekas (76) to break up a pass by quarterback Ed Brown (15) late in the second quarter.

▼ New coach Vince Lombardi is carried off the field by his players after the Packers beat the Chicago Bears 9-7 in the season opener on Sept. 27, 1959. Closest to Lombardi, from left, are Max McGee (85), Bobby Dillon (44), Bill Quinlan (83), Lew Carpenter (33), Don McIlhenny (42) and Paul Hornung (5).

SEPT. 27, 1959
A NEW ERA BEGINS
PACKERS 9, BEARS 7

Little did anyone know that this game would be a sign of things to come. The Packers carry their new coach, Vince Lombardi, off the field following a come-from-behind victory sparked by a Jim Taylor touchdown and a Dave Hanner safety.

Dec. 31, 1961
Golden game
Packers 37, Giants 0

Paul Hornung, on leave from the Army, scores 19 points in the first NFL title game in Green Bay. The Packers score 24 second-quarter points against the league's top-rated defense. They also intercept four Giants passes. The championship is the first of five that the team will win under coach Vince Lombardi.

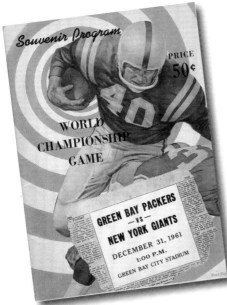

▶ Packers fans hold up a sign with what appears to be a huge ring of bologna on one side and the phrase "Giant Meat" on the other side.

▶ From left, New York Giants president Jack Mara, NFL commissioner Pete Rozelle and Packers president Dominic Olejniczak examine the playing field the day before the game.

▲ Linebacker Ray Nitschke (66) and an unidentified teammate haul down Giants fullback Alex Webster (29) late in the second quarter. Defensive back John Symank (27) closes in on the play at left.

▲ Harold Baker, a vendor at City Stadium, sits on his case of Pabst Blue Ribbon beer and watches part of the NFL championship game against the New York Giants on Dec. 31, 1961. A bottle of Pabst went for 35 cents.

▲ Tight end Ron Kramer (88) knocks over three New York Giants players, including linebacker Sam Huff (70) and defensive back Joe Morrison (40), on his way to the end zone for one of his two touchdowns. Max McGee (85) watches at left.

▲ Coach Vince Lombardi is carried off the field by linebacker Dan Currie, center, and defensive tackle Dave Hanner, right. Fullback Jim Taylor is at left.

◀ Quarterback Bart Starr, left, and tight end Ron Kramer celebrate in the shower after the Packers' victory.

Dec. 26, 1965
The Kick, Part I
Packers 13, Colts 10, overtime

Packers win the Western Conference title against the mighty Colts in a special playoff game because both teams finished at 10-3-1. The Colts are quarterbacked by running back Tom Matte in an emergency role. Don Chandler wins it with a 25-yard field goal in sudden-death overtime. His 22-yarder, tying the game with 1:58 left in regulation, sparks controversy. The kick sails above the tips of the uprights, making it difficult to judge whether it was good. The next season, the league increases the height of goal posts.

◀ Ticket stub from Packers-Colts playoff game, Dec. 26, 1965.

▼ The Packers' defense converges on Colts quarterback Tom Matte (41). Clockwise from upper left are linebacker Ray Nitschke (66), defensive tackle Henry Jordan (74), defensive end Lionel Aldridge (82) and linebacker Lee Roy Caffey (60).

▲ Program from Packers-Colts playoff game, Dec. 26, 1965.

▲ Quarterback Bart Starr lies on the field after injuring his ribs while trying to stop Colts linebacker Don Shinnick from scoring on a 25-yard fumble return on the Packers' first play from scrimmage.

▼ Bart Starr (15) is helped off the field by guard Jerry Kramer (64) and Dr. James Nellen, the team's physician.

▲ With injured quarterback Bart Starr holding, Don Chandler (34) kicks the game-winning field goal in overtime. Colts linebacker Don Shinnick (66) tries for the block.

▲ Running back Jim Taylor's No. 31 is covered with mud as he's gang-tackled by the Browns. Guard Jerry Kramer (64) and tight end Bill Anderson (88) are on the ground.

▼ Linebacker Ray Nitschke (66) and cornerback Bob Jeter (21) close in on Browns running back Jim Brown late in the second quarter. It was Brown's last game. He retired after the season to pursue an acting career.

Jan. 2, 1966
The sweep
Packers 23, Browns 12

The Packers win their first of three consecutive NFL titles on a snowy, mud-soaked field, holding league rushing leader Jim Brown to 50 yards. The Packers put the game away with a 90-yard, third-quarter drive, culminating with a famous touchdown sweep as Paul Hornung slips and slides into the corner of the end zone.

◀ Fans try to tear down the last remaining piece of the goal post in the south end zone after the Packers' victory.

▲ Cornerback Herb Adderley (26) and safety Willie Wood, in T-shirt, are interviewed by CBS' Ray Scott in the locker room after the game.

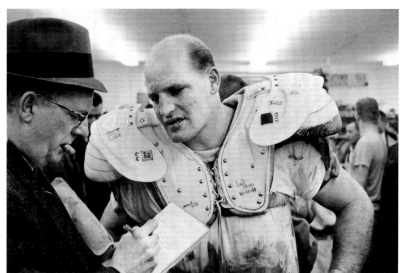

▲ Still wearing his shoulder pads, linebacker Ray Nitschke talks to Chicago Sun-Times reporter Bill Gleason in the locker room after the game.

◀ Guard Fuzzy Thurston enjoys a victory cigar while talking to Baltimore News-Post sports editor John Steadman in the locker room.

▶ Surrounded by reporters, coach Vince Lombardi meets the media in the locker room after the game.

SEPT. 7, 1980
KICK AND CATCH
PACKERS 12, BEARS 6

Six minutes into overtime, Chester Marcol catches his own blocked field-goal try and runs 25 yards for the game-winning touchdown. It's the only overtime game in the storied Packers-Bears rivalry — one of the longest in NFL history.

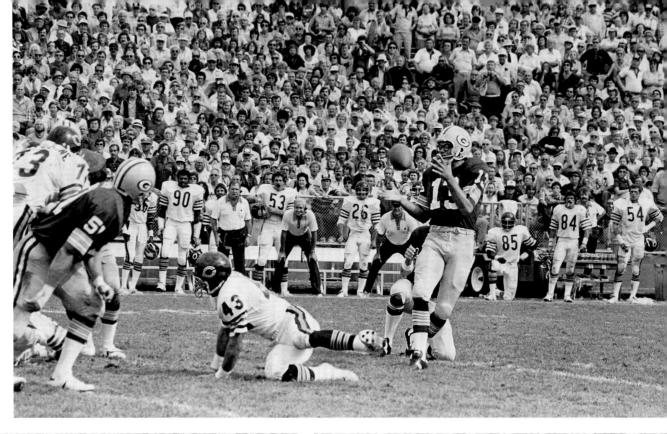

▶ The ball caroms back to kicker Chester Marcol after being blocked. Marcol caught the ball and ran for the winning touchdown.

▼ The Bears' Doug Plank (46) and Mike Ulmer (43) are among those giving chase as Marcol runs toward the end zone.

▲ A delighted coach Bart Starr heads toward the locker room after Marcol's touchdown gave the Packers the victory on opening day.

JAN. 8, 1983

BACK TO THE PLAYOFFS
PACKERS 41, CARDINALS 16

For the first time in 15 years, Lambeau Field hosts a postseason game. Quarterback Lynn Dickey throws four touchdown passes, tying the Packers' playoff record set by Bart Starr in 1967. Wide receivers John Jefferson and James Lofton carve up the St. Louis secondary. The Packers' 41 points are a team playoff record.

◀ Packers players sit in a makeshift shelter along the sideline during the game. Seated from left are tackle Tim Stokes (76), guard Leotis Harris (69), tackle Angelo Fields (79) and tight end John Thompson (87). The temperature was 20 degrees at kickoff, and although 54,282 attended, the game didn't sell out — the first time that had happened since a regular-season game against Washington in 1959.

▲ Program from Packers-Cardinals playoff game, Jan. 8, 1983.

◀ Fans fill the field and start to tear down the goal posts after the Packers' victory.

▲ Wide receiver James Lofton (80) gets ready to receive a high five from wide receiver John Jefferson (83) after scoring a second-quarter touchdown.

Oct. 17, 1983
Monday night shootout
Packers 48, Redskins 47

The two teams combine for a scoring record in a Monday night game as the Packers beat the defending Super Bowl champions. Green Bay quarterback Lynn Dickey passes for 387 yards, fifth-highest in team history. It is the highest-scoring game in Packers history.

▶ Defensive end Byron Braggs (73) and running back Gerry Ellis (31) get in on the high fives after the Packers' victory. It was one of the most thrilling Monday night games in NFL history.

▶ Running back Gerry Ellis breaks into the clear with Washington cornerback Darrell Green (28) and safety Mark Murphy (29) among those in pursuit. Ellis had a couple of big plays in the game: a 24-yard touchdown run in the third quarter and a 56-yard pass from quarterback Lynn Dickey that he caught near midfield. Ellis outran the defense before being caught by Green, then a rookie, at the Washington 8. That set up Jan Stenerud's game-winning field goal from 20 yards out with 54 seconds left. Washington's Mark Moseley missed a 39-yard field-goal try with just 3 seconds left. *Photo from Green Bay Packers archive*

> *One memory is the Monday Night game against the Washington Redskins. The stadium was just packed, seemed like more people were in there than you could get in. There was an electricity in the air that night.*
>
> *"You walk out there and the people are so close, they're above you along the sidelines. It seemed like a small stadium compared to some of the others we played in, but the fans made it seem like one of the biggest once they got going."*
>
> **— Paul Coffman, Packers tight end, 1978-85**

▲ The nasty weather didn't deter these fans.

▶ Wide receiver Phillip Epps dives for, but just misses, a pass from quarterback Lynn Dickey. Buccaneers cornerback Jeremiah Castille (23) defends on the play.

DEC. 1, 1985
THE SNOW BOWL
PACKERS 21, BUCCANEERS 0

Warm-weather Tampa Bay manages only five first downs and 11 passing yards in a blinding blizzard that limits the Lambeau Field crowd to 19,856. Road conditions are so bad — aggravated by a foot of wet, heavy snow and 30-mph winds — that some fans arrive by snowmobile.

▲ It took four Buccaneers to bring down running back Eddie Lee Ivery.

▼ Tight end Paul Coffman (82) said this game was the only time he ever outran a defensive back.

▲ There were plenty of empty seats on Dec. 1, 1985, when only 19,856 could get to the stadium.

Nov. 5, 1989
After further review ...
Packers 14, Bears 13

With the fierce rivalry between the Packers and Bears at its peak, Green Bay ends an eight-game losing streak to Chicago when Don Majkowski hits Sterling Sharpe for the apparent game-winning touchdown in the waning moments. Majkowski, however, is flagged for crossing the line of scrimmage, but a review by instant replay reverses the decision.

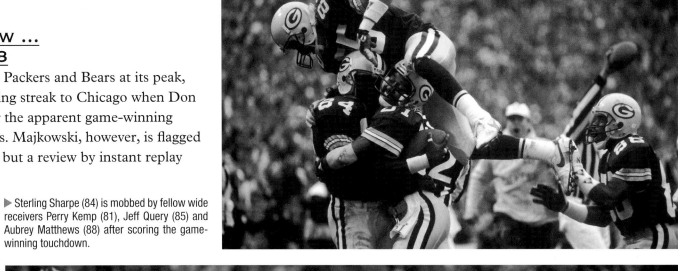

▶ Sterling Sharpe (84) is mobbed by fellow wide receivers Perry Kemp (81), Jeff Query (85) and Aubrey Matthews (88) after scoring the game-winning touchdown.

SEC. 04 ROW 57 SEAT 24

PACKERS
VS.
BEARS

November 5, 1989

▲ Ticket stub from Packers-Bears game, Nov. 5, 1989.

▲ Packers quarterback Don Majkowski (7) celebrates the instant-replay call confirming his game-winning touchdown pass to Sterling Sharpe. Also celebrating are wide receiver Perry Kemp (81), running back Herman Fontenot (27) and linebacker Johnny Holland (50).

SEPT. 20, 1992
CALL IT FORESHADOWING
PACKERS 24, BENGALS 23

New coach Mike Holmgren's team is losing 20-7. Backup quarterback Brett Favre comes off the bench to lead the Packers to a come-from-behind victory. With 13 seconds remaining, Favre completes a 35-yard touchdown pass to Kitrick Taylor. Favre starts the next week and stays at quarterback for the next decade and beyond.

◀ Quarterback Don Majkowski (7) writhes in pain after straining ligaments in his left ankle while being sacked by Bengals nose tackle Tim Krumrie (69) during the first quarter. Tackle Tootie Robbins (73) stands over Majkowski, who left the game and was replaced — permanently, as it turned out — by Brett Favre.

▲ Ticket stub from Packers-Bengals game, Sept. 20, 1992.

▲ Center James Campen hugs coach Mike Holmgren, who's drenched in Gatorade. It was Holmgren's first victory as the Packers' coach.

◀ Brett Favre celebrates after Chris Jacke's extra point capped the Packers' victory over the Cincinnati Bengals. Favre took over as the starter the next week and never left.

> From the first time I played against Cincinnati, I thought it was an honor then to play at Lambeau Field, and that hasn't changed. It's just got a little bit better. One thing that hasn't changed is the fans.
> "For a small town, you ride around and go, 'They can't fill this stadium.' But there's a huge waiting list and the fans are great. So every time I step on the field, I do appreciate and realize that being able to do that is something special. "
>
> — Brett Favre, Packers quarterback, 1992-present

Oct. 10, 1993

REG-GIE! REG-GIE! REG-GIE!
PACKERS 30, BRONCOS 27

Defensive end Reggie White, who shocked the NFL by signing with Green Bay as a free agent during the offseason, sacks John Elway on third and fourth down late in the fourth quarter to stop the Broncos' last drive at the Packers' 43-yard line. Elway almost single-handedly kept Denver in the game, completing 33 of 59 passes. White had five tackles and three sacks in the game.

> You can't convince me that there is a better tradition with another team than here. There is something special about playing in Green Bay, and as an athlete being able to play for the Green Bay Packers, and then win a championship while you are a Green Bay Packer, it just doesn't get better than that.
>
> "I've told people if you want to have a football experience, a great football experience, you have to watch a game at Lambeau."
>
> — *Reggie White, Packers defensive end, 1993-98*

▶ Defensive end Reggie White looks down at John Elway after sacking the Broncos quarterback late in the game, thwarting Denver's drive for what might have been a game-winning touchdown. The back-to-back sacks drew thunderous "Reg-gie! Reg-gie! Reg-gie!" chants from the Lambeau Field crowd. *Harmann Studios photo from Green Bay Packers archive*

▲ Defensive end Reggie White (92) looks up at safety LeRoy Butler (36), to whom he's just lateraled the ball after being caught by Raiders tackle Steve Wisniewski (76) while returning a fumble. Linebacker Bryce Paup (95) is on the ground. Butler took it in for a touchdown, then delivered the first Lambeau Leap.

▼ Fans embrace Butler as he does the first Lambeau Leap, going into the stands beyond the south end zone after going 25 yards to score on a lateral from White. *Harmann Studios photo from Green Bay Packers archive*

DEC. 26, 1993
THE BIRTH OF THE LAMBEAU LEAP
PACKERS 28, RAIDERS 0

On a bitterly cold day when the temperature at kickoff is zero, LeRoy Butler starts a Green Bay tradition with an impromptu jump into the south stands after scoring a fourth-quarter touchdown. He takes a lateral from Reggie White, who'd recovered Randy Jordan's fumble at the Los Angeles 35-yard line, and returns it 25 yards for the score.

▲ The game well in hand, safeties LeRoy Butler (36) and George Teague (31) sit on the Packers' bench.

DEC. 31, 1994
NOWHERE TO RUN
PACKERS 16, LIONS 12

The Packers shut down Detroit running back Barry Sanders, the NFL rushing leader. Fritz Shurmur's defense holds Sanders to minus-1 yard on 13 attempts. The victory gives the Packers their second straight NFC wild-card playoff win over the Lions.

▲ Ticket stub from Packers-Lions playoff game, Dec. 31, 1994.

▲ Defensive tackle Don Davey wraps up Lions running back Barry Sanders. Lions center Kevin Glover (53) blocks at left as linebacker George Koonce (53) closes in on the play. *Harmann Studios photo from Green Bay Packers archive*

CHRISTMAS COMES EARLY
PACKERS 24, STEELERS 19

The Packers clinch their first NFC Central Division title in 23 years when Pittsburgh receiver Yancey Thigpen drops an almost certain game-winning touchdown pass in the northwest corner of the end zone with just 11 seconds left in the game.

▲ One of the Packers' greatest moments came courtesy of Pittsburgh Steelers receiver Yancey Thigpen, whose dropped pass in the northwest corner of the end zone on Christmas Eve 1995 helped clinch Green Bay's first NFC Central Division title since 1972.

◄ Packers safety George Teague (31) has a word with Thigpen after the Steelers receiver dropped what would have been the game-winning touchdown pass.

◄ Ticket stub from Packers-Steelers game, Dec. 24, 1995.

Oct. 14, 1996
THE KICK, PART II
PACKERS 23, 49ERS 20 (OT)

The Packers rally before a national TV audience with a late game-tying field goal, followed by the game-winner by Chris Jacke from 53 yards out — the longest overtime field goal in league history. The Monday night win proves pivotal in helping the Packers claim home-field advantage en route to their Super Bowl XXXI victory.

▶ Don Beebe hauls in a pass. Playing in place of the injured Robert Brooks, the veteran Beebe had 11 catches for 220 yards and a touchdown.

▼ Chris Jacke (13) follows through on his game-winning 53-yard field goal in overtime. Craig Hentrich (17) is the holder.

▲ Quarterback Brett Favre, left, hugs defensive end Reggie White after the Packers beat the 49ers.

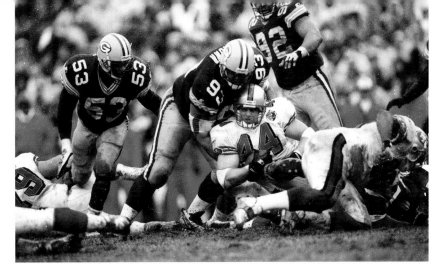

▶ Nose tackle Gilbert Brown (93) stops 49ers running back Tommy Vardell (44) as linebacker George Koonce (53) and defensive end Reggie White (92) close in.

JAN. 4, 1997
THE MUD BOWL
PACKERS 35, 49ERS 14

The Packers' Desmond Howard electrifies the crowd with two key punt returns in a driving rainstorm in the NFC divisional playoff game. Despite the dismal conditions, there are only a reported three no-shows among a crowd of 60,787. The field is turned into a quagmire by the game's end, requiring new sod for the next week's game.

▲ Desmond Howard is buried by fans and teammates Roderick Mullen (28), Keith McKenzie (95), Terry Mickens (85) and Jeff Thomason (83) after a Lambeau Leap capping his 71-yard punt return for a touchdown early in the first quarter.

◀ The torn-up field behind defensive end Sean Jones shows why this game was called the Mud Bowl.

Jan. 12, 1997
BACK TO THE SUPER BOWL
PACKERS 30, PANTHERS 13

The Packers earn their first trip to the Super Bowl in 29 seasons as Dorsey Levens accounts for a combined 205 yards in rushing and receiving in the NFC Championship Game. The game-time temperature is 3, with a wind chill of minus-17. Despite the bitter weather, the crowd stays for a postgame ceremony at midfield and cheers the team for 30 minutes.

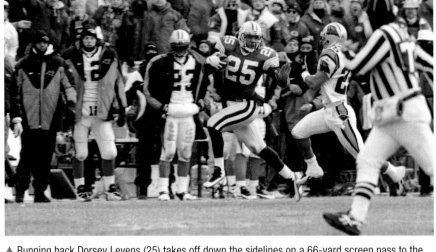

▲ Running back Dorsey Levens (25) takes off down the sidelines on a 66-yard screen pass to the Carolina 4-yard line early in the third quarter. The Packers scored on the next play to make it 27-13.

◄ Panthers safety Chad Cota winces in the cold.

▲ It may have been 3 degrees at kickoff, with a wind chill of 17 below, but it didn't bother Packers fans.

► From left, Adam Timmerman (63), Mark Chmura (89), Antonio Freeman (86) and Don Beebe (82) celebrate the Packers' victory.

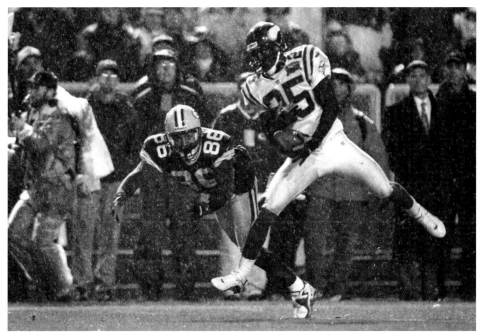

NOV. 6, 2000
THE CATCH
PACKERS 26, MINNESOTA 20

In another overtime classic on a rainy Monday night, Brett Favre launches a pass to Antonio Freeman. The ball bounces off defender Cris Dishman's body. Freeman slips and is lying on his stomach, but juggles the ball off his body. The ball never touches the ground, so Freeman gets up, runs into the end zone untouched and scores the game-winning 43-yard touchdown.

Antonio Freeman's game-winning touchdown catch and run.

CHAPTER FOUR

UNFORGETTABLE PLAYERS

The new brick warehouse-style façade at renovated Lambeau Field is so appropriate. Memories are stored there, after all.

Dating to 1957, these memories are like often-told family stories. They linger in the old bowl, waiting to be taken out and dusted off anytime Packers fans reminisce.

More than any stadium in the NFL, Lambeau Field honors the past. The four retired numbers and the names of team members inducted in the Pro Football Hall of Fame recall Packers legends from the earliest days of professional football.

In the past four-plus decades, more of the game's most unforgettable players have cast their shadows on the turf of Lambeau Field than on any other field in the league.

The players most often recalled by Packers fans wore the green and gold. But opposing players also came to Green Bay to write their own chapters of Lambeau Field history.

Packers fans have long memories of great players and great games, but, as the years pass, the mind's images begin to fade. The renovation of Lambeau Field, from keeping the bowl to building the new Packers Hall of Fame, preserves a place for fans to keep their memories stored: 1265 Lombardi Ave.

◀ Fullback John Brockington sheds Chargers defensive lineman Dave Tipton and heads upfield during the Packers' 34-0 victory over San Diego on Nov. 24, 1974. Quarterback John Hadl and tackle Dick Himes (72) watch from behind the play.

▶ From left, halfback Paul Hornung (5), fullback Jim Taylor (31), wide receiver Max McGee (85) and quarterback Bart Starr (15) sit on the sidelines during a 49-0 victory over the Chicago Bears on Sept. 30, 1962.

FOUR RETIRED NUMBERS

Don Hutson, Tony Canadeo, Bart Starr, Ray Nitschke. The mere sight of the names of these Packers legends should intimidate opposing players who dare tread on the sod of Lambeau Field.

That's the theory behind one of the crowning touches of the Lambeau Field renovation: the addition of the names of the four Packers players whose jersey numbers have been retired. Placed in the north end zone, those names and numbers are among the first sights for opposing players as they emerge from the visiting team's tunnel.

The careers of Canadeo and Hutson predate Lambeau Field. Starr played his first season at old City Stadium and the rest of his career at Lambeau. Nitschke played his entire career at Lambeau.

The ceremonies saluting the end of Starr's and Nitschke's playing careers are among the most memorable ever held at Lambeau Field.

DON HUTSON
END ~ 1935-45

Hutson is credited with no less than inventing pass patterns. He led the league in receiving for eight years and in scoring for five years. He also played defensive back and kicker. His league record for most points scored in a quarter — 29 — stood into the 21st century. He was named to the NFL's all-50-year team in 1970 and to its 75th-anniversary and all-time two-way teams in 1994.

The Packers retired Hutson's jersey number, 14, in 1951.

TONY CANADEO
HALFBACK ~ 1941-44, 1946-52

Fifty years after he retired, Canadeo still ranked as the third-leading ground gainer in Packers history, with 4,197 yards in 1,025 attempts, a 4.1-yard average. He was a good blocker and receiver, not to mention a capable passer and kick returner. He also played defensive back early in his career.

The Packers retired Canadeo's jersey number, 3, in 1952.

BART STARR
QUARTERBACK ~ 1956-71

On Oct. 18, 1970, a sun-swept Sunday at Lambeau Field, quarterback Bart Starr accepted an outpouring of gratitude from 56,263 fans. Flanked by former Glory Years teammates at a halftime ceremony, Starr received a special telegram from Western Union with more than 40,000 names from Packers fans all over the country. After the 31-21 loss to the Los Angeles Rams that day, Starr was asked whether the festivities took a toll. "There were distractions, sure," he said. "But you just have to take those things in stride and overcome them." On the day before the tribute, President Nixon came to town. Praising Starr, the president said, "He's not only the No. 1 pro quarterback, he's also a No. 1 American."

The Packers retired Starr's jersey number, 15, in 1973.

RAY NITSCHKE
LINEBACKER ~ 1958-72

The big guy cried on Dec. 12, 1971, just before the Packers took on the Chicago Bears. It was Ray Nitschke Day. During the pregame festivities, Nitschke, one of the most intense linebackers ever to play the game, stood on the Lambeau Field turf and wiped tears from his eyes with his large, taped-up hands. Nitschke, 34, relegated to a backup role for most of the season, played the entire game, which the Packers won 31-10. Later he said, "This has been a wonderful day, Dec. 12, 1971 ... beating the Chicago Bears."

The Packers retired Nitschke's jersey number, 66, in 1983.

◀ Two of the greatest Packers of all time — end Don Hutson (14) and running back Tony Canadeo (3) — played together for four seasons, from 1941 to 1944. Both men are in the Pro Football Hall of Fame. Their numbers are two of the four retired by the Packers.

BART STARR

► Quarterback Bart Starr (15) confers with coach Vince Lombardi on the sidelines during a 9-7 victory over the Detroit Lions on Oct. 7, 1962.

▲ Program from Bart Starr Day, Oct. 18, 1970.

► Starr bows his head during a moment of silence for former coach Vince Lombardi, who is dying of cancer, as the Packers host the New York Giants in a preseason game on Aug. 8, 1970. Lombardi died three weeks later in Washington, D.C.

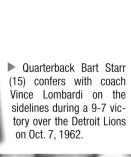

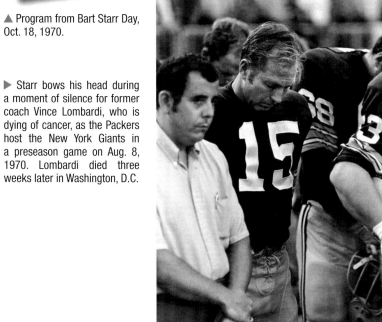

▲ An emotional Starr greets his 1962 teammates during Bart Starr Day on Oct. 18, 1970, at halftime of the game against the Los Angeles Rams. He's surrounded by Paul Hornung (5), Max McGee, Bob Skoronski (76) and Dan Currie (58).

► Starr acknowledges tributes on Bart Starr Day. From left, he's flanked by former teammates Bob Skoronski (76), Paul Hornung (5), Max McGee (85), Jim Taylor (31) and Hank Gremminger (46).

RAY NITSCHKE

▲ Card from Ray Nitschke Day, Dec. 12, 1971.

▶ Ray Nitschke kisses his wife, Jackie, during ceremonies on Ray Nitschke Day, Dec. 12, 1971, before the game against the Chicago Bears.

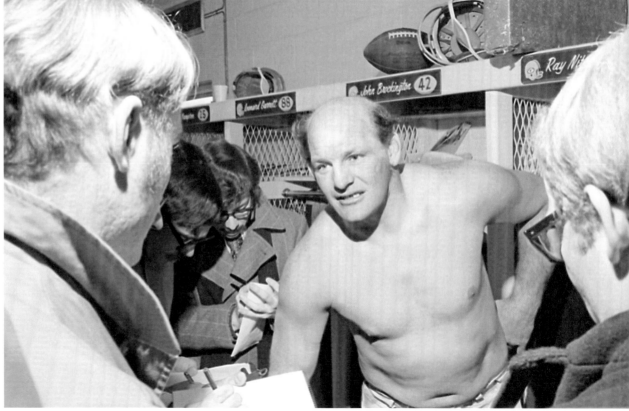

▶ Ray Nitschke talks to reporters after the Packers beat the Chicago Bears 31-10 on Ray Nitschke Day.

▲ Nitschke wipes away a tear as he listens to the ovation from Packers fans during ceremonies on Ray Nitschke Day.

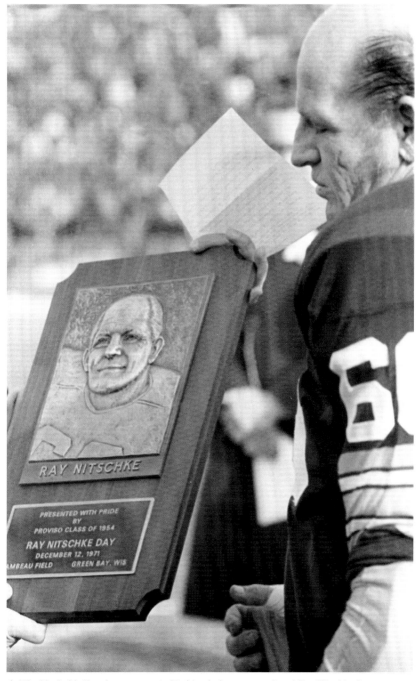

▲ Nitschke holds the plaque presented to him during ceremonies at Ray Nitschke Day.

Henry Jordan

DT, 1959-69
Pro Hall of Fame: 1995
Started career with Cleveland. All-Pro five straight seasons. Colorful personality. Missed only two games in his first 12 seasons. Played in seven NFL title games, including one with Cleveland.

Don Hutson

E/DB, 1935-45
Pro Hall of Fame: 1963
Credited with inventing pass patterns. Led league in receiving eight years and scoring five years. One of league's all-time leaders in touchdown receptions (99). Named to league's 75th Anniversary and All-Time Two-Way teams in 1994.

Johnny (Blood) McNally

HB, 1929-33, 1935-36
Pro Hall of Fame: 1963
A gifted runner and receiver. Played role in Packers' first four championships: 1929, 1930, 1931 and 1936.

Vince Lombardi

Coach, 1959-67
Pro Hall of Fame: 1971
Led Packers to unparalleled five NFL championships in seven years: 1961, 1962, 1965, 1966 and 1967, the latter two championships followed by wins in the first two Super Bowls. Never had a losing season. Compiled overall record of 98-30-4.

Ray Nitschke

MLB, 1958-72
Pro Hall of Fame: 1978
Personified the warrior spirit in the blood-and-guts NFL of the 1960s. Renowned as a fearless hitter. All-Pro 1964-66. Named to league's 75th Anniversary Team. Played in 190 games.

Jim Taylor

FB, 1958-66
Pro Hall of Fame: 1976
Rushed for more than 1,000 yards five straight seasons. Scored 83 rushing touchdowns with Packers and New Orleans Saints (1967). Is Packers' all-time rushing leader with 8,207 yards in nine seasons. Had 26 career 100-yard rushing games.

Tony Canadeo

HB, 1941-44, 1946-52
Pro Hall of Fame: 1974
Became only third 1,000-yard rusher in league history when he gained 1,052 yards in 1949. Accomplished as a blocker, passer, receiver and kick returner. Also played defensive back early in his career. Nicknamed "Grey Ghost" from his college career at Gonzaga.

Earl L. (Curly) Lambeau

Founder, coach, 1919-49
Pro Hall of Fame: 1963
Played halfback until 1929, pioneering the forward pass in pro football. Led Packers to six world championships. Compiled coaching record of 212-106-21 with the Packers.

Arnie Herber

QB, 1930-40
Pro Hall of Fame: 1966
Pro football's first great long passer, teaming with Don Hutson. Won NFL passing titles in 1932, 1934 and 1936. Threw 66 touchdown passes as a Packer. Also an accomplished punter.

Willie Davis

DE, 1960-69
Pro Hall of Fame: 1981
One of premier pass rushers in league history. Recovered 21 fumbles. All-Pro five times. Helped Packers win five NFL titles. Elected to Packers Board of Directors in 1994.

Bart Starr

QB, 1956-71
Pro Hall of Fame: 1977
Led Packers to five world titles. Named MVP of Super Bowls I and II. Led league in passing in 1962, 1964 and 1966. Played in 196 games. Also was head coach of the Packers, 1975-83.

Paul Hornung

HB, 1957-62, 1964-66
Pro Hall of Fame: 1986
Heisman Trophy winner at Notre Dame. Won NFL scoring title three straight years, 1959-61. Model of versatility, averaging 4.2 yards per rush, catching 130 passes and kicking 66 field goals in his career. Scored 33 points vs. Baltimore Colts, Oct. 8, 1961.

The renovation preserves the stadium bowl, which includes a display of the names and seasons played or coached by Packers greats inducted into the Pro Football Hall of Fame.

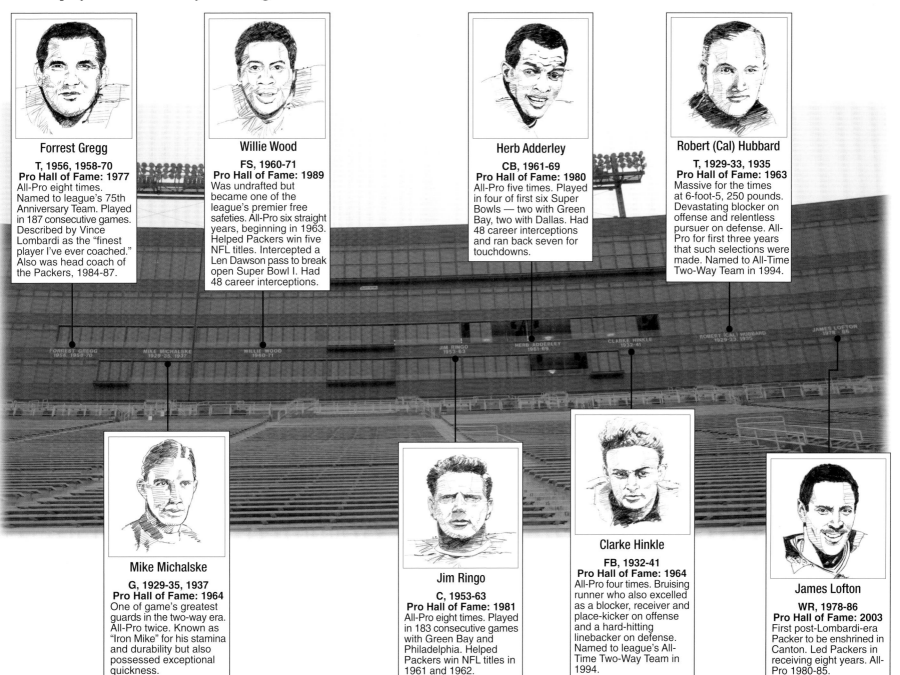

Forrest Gregg

T, 1956, 1958-70
Pro Hall of Fame: 1977
All-Pro eight times. Named to league's 75th Anniversary Team. Played in 187 consecutive games. Described by Vince Lombardi as the "finest player I've ever coached." Also was head coach of the Packers, 1984-87.

Willie Wood

FS, 1960-71
Pro Hall of Fame: 1989
Was undrafted but became one of the league's premier free safeties. All-Pro six straight years, beginning in 1963. Helped Packers win five NFL titles. Intercepted a Len Dawson pass to break open Super Bowl I. Had 48 career interceptions.

Herb Adderley

CB, 1961-69
Pro Hall of Fame: 1980
All-Pro five times. Played in four of first six Super Bowls — two with Green Bay, two with Dallas. Had 48 career interceptions and ran back seven for touchdowns.

Robert (Cal) Hubbard

T, 1929-33, 1935
Pro Hall of Fame: 1963
Massive for the times at 6-foot-5, 250 pounds. Devastating blocker on offense and relentless pursuer on defense. All-Pro for first three years that such selections were made. Named to All-Time Two-Way Team in 1994.

Mike Michalske

G, 1929-35, 1937
Pro Hall of Fame: 1964
One of game's greatest guards in the two-way era. All-Pro twice. Known as "Iron Mike" for his stamina and durability but also possessed exceptional quickness.

Jim Ringo

C, 1953-63
Pro Hall of Fame: 1981
All-Pro eight times. Played in 183 consecutive games with Green Bay and Philadelphia. Helped Packers win NFL titles in 1961 and 1962.

Clarke Hinkle

FB, 1932-41
Pro Hall of Fame: 1964
All-Pro four times. Bruising runner who also excelled as a blocker, receiver and place-kicker on offense and a hard-hitting linebacker on defense. Named to league's All-Time Two-Way Team in 1994.

James Lofton

WR, 1978-86
Pro Hall of Fame: 2003
First post-Lombardi-era Packer to be enshrined in Canton. Led Packers in receiving eight years. All-Pro 1980-85.

MORE UNFORGETTABLE PACKERS

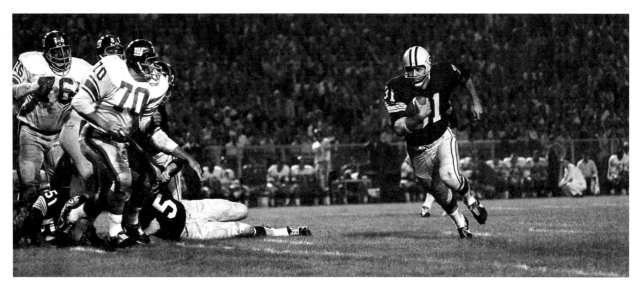

▲ Defensive back Bobby Dillon (44) returns an interception 37 yards for the first touchdown in the Packers' 34-20 loss to the Chicago Bears on Sept. 28, 1958. Rookie linebacker Ray Nitschke (33) fends off Bears quarterback Ed Brown (15), while defensive tackle Dave Hanner (79) runs with Dillon. It was the only year Nitschke wore No. 33; he switched to his familiar No. 66 in 1959.

▲ Fullback Jim Taylor (31) heads upfield during a preseason game against the New York Giants on Sept. 3, 1962. Giants defensive tackle Rosey Grier (76) and linebacker Sam Huff (70) give chase. The Packers won 20-17.

▼ Cornerback Herb Adderley (26) tries to block a kick by the New York Giants' Don Chandler (34) during a preseason game on Sept. 3, 1962.

▲ It takes three Lions — defensive end Darris McCord (78) and linebackers Carl Brettschneider (57) and Joe Schmidt (56) — to haul down fullback Jim Taylor (31) during a 9-7 victory over Detroit on Oct. 7, 1962.

▲ Halfback Paul Hornung (5) steps into the end zone for a touchdown during a 34-7 victory over the Minnesota Vikings in the season opener on Sept. 16, 1962. Trailing on the play at right are tackle Bob Skoronski (76) and guard Jerry Kramer (64), who keeps Vikings linebacker Rip Hawkins (58) at bay.

▲ Packers coach Vince Lombardi looks on from the sidelines during a game against the Baltimore Colts on Sept. 20, 1964. The Packers lost 21-20.

◄ Lombardi, center, praises his players for a job well done in a 42-10 victory over the Los Angeles Rams on Oct. 6, 1963. Defensive coordinator Phil Bengtson is at left.

▶ Halfback Paul Hornung (5) heads upfield during a 49-0 victory over the Chicago Bears on Sept. 30, 1962. One Packers lineman blocks Bears defensive back J.C. Caroline (25), and guard Jerry Kramer (64) stops Bears defensive tackle Maury Youmans (82).

▼ San Francisco running back Ken Willard hits the left side of the line for no gain, running into defensive end Willie Davis (87), linebacker Ray Nitschke (66) and defensive back Tom Brown (40) as the Packers' defense makes a goal-line stand during a 27-10 victory over the 49ers on Oct. 10, 1965.

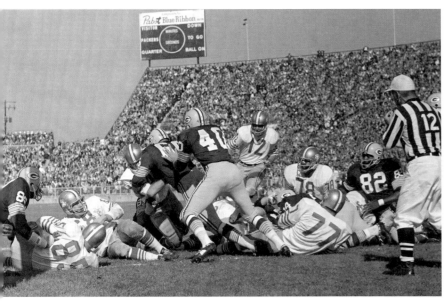

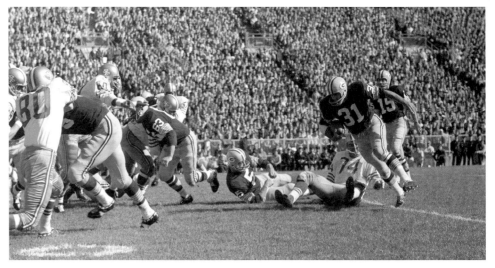

▲ Fullback Jim Taylor (31) leaves San Francisco defensive end Clark Miller (74) in his wake as he runs a sweep to the left during a 27-10 victory over the 49ers on Oct. 10, 1965.

▲ Defensive end Willie Davis (87) puts pressure on Philadelphia quarterback King Hill (10) during a victory over the Eagles on Sept. 15, 1968. At right, defensive end Lionel Aldridge (82) is blocked by Eagles center Gene Ceppetelli (54).

▲ Running back Travis Williams (23) turns upfield during a 17-0 victory over the Chicago Bears in the season opener on Sept. 21, 1969. Guard Bill Lueck (62) leads the blocking while Bears defensive end Lloyd Phillips (86) pursues.

▲ Phil Bengtson strikes a characteristic pose, cigarette in hand, during his regular-season coaching debut against the Philadelphia Eagles on Sept. 15, 1968. The Packers won 30-13.

◀ Coach Dan Devine lies on the field, his leg broken after being run over on the sidelines by Giants center Bob Hyland — a former Packer — during the season opener against New York on Sept. 19, 1971.

❝ *The fans make Lambeau Field special. That gives you so much energy and a sense of purpose to play and win. And when you win you know you have created satisfaction for the fans beyond most other things they will do in the course of the week. When you played there, at least for me, you experienced the thrill of victory with your teammates and almost as much through the reaction of the fans.*❞

— Willie Davis, Packers defensive end, 1960-69

▲ Quarterback Lynn Dickey rests on the bench during the Packers' 23-20 victory over the New York Giants in the home opener on Sept. 15, 1985.

▲ Linebacker Mike Douglass exhales steam as he watches the final minutes of the Packers' 34-24 loss to the Miami Dolphins on Dec. 8, 1985. The temperature was 23 degrees at kickoff.

▲ From left, linebackers Randy Scott and Rich Wingo and tight end Paul Coffman slide in the mud to celebrate the Packers' 27-14 victory over the Tampa Bay Buccaneers on Dec. 2, 1984.

▲ Cornerback Tim Lewis is carried off the field on a stretcher after a head-to-head collision with Bears wide receiver Willie Gault during the Packers' 25-12 loss to Chicago on Sept. 22, 1986. Lewis sustained a career-ending neck injury.

▲ Wide receiver James Lofton leaps above Lions defensive back Duane Galloway to score a touchdown during the second quarter of the Packers' 21-14 loss to Detroit on Oct. 12, 1986.

◄ Wide receiver James Lofton holds aloft a game ball given to him at Lambeau Field on Oct. 12, 1986, to commemorate his record for career pass receptions, set the week before in a game against the Cincinnati Bengals at Milwaukee County Stadium. Lofton, who was traded from the Packers to the Los Angeles Raiders in 1987, was inducted into the Pro Football Hall of Fame in 2003.

▲ Defensive line coach Greg Blache buries his face in the grass after Tampa Bay's Willie Drewrey turned a deflected pass into an 87-yard touchdown during the fourth quarter of the Packers' 15-13 victory over the Buccaneers on Sept. 15, 1991.

▼ Linebacker Tim Harris pulls the trigger with both hands, celebrating a second-quarter sack of Rams quarterback Jim Everett during the Packers' 36-24 season-opening victory over Los Angeles on Sept. 9, 1990.

▲ Defensive end Reggie White stands in the north end zone, waiting to be introduced before the Packers' game against the Minnesota Vikings on Sept. 21, 1997. He's flanked by photographers and game-day personnel.

◄ Retired defensive end Reggie White pauses to compose himself as he is honored during ceremonies at halftime of the Packers' game against the Tampa Bay Buccaneers on Oct. 10, 1999. Although his No. 92 jersey wasn't officially retired, it — like Paul Hornung's No. 5 — seems unlikely to be reissued with any regularity. White came out of retirement to play one more season, for the Carolina Panthers, in 2000.

Unforgettable Opponents

▲ Chicago Bears coach George Halas looks on from the sidelines during a 49-0 loss to the Packers on Sept. 30, 1962. Behind him are guard Stan Jones, also kneeling, and assistants Sid Luckman and Phil Handler.

▼ Giants halfback Frank Gifford (16) tries to fend off defensive tackle Henry Jordan (74) during the second quarter of a preseason game on Sept. 3, 1962. Gifford was dropped for a 10-yard loss on the play. The Packers beat the Giants 20-17.

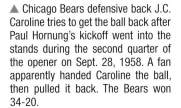

▲ Chicago Bears defensive back J.C. Caroline tries to get the ball back after Paul Hornung's kickoff went into the stands during the second quarter of the opener on Sept. 28, 1958. A fan apparently handed Caroline the ball, then pulled it back. The Bears won 34-20.

▶ Chicago Bears running back Gale Sayers (40) follows guard George Seals (67) into the heart of the Green Bay defense during a 17-0 loss to the Packers in the season opener on Sept. 21, 1969. Defensive end Willie Davis (87) and linebacker Dave Robinson (89) try to stop Sayers.

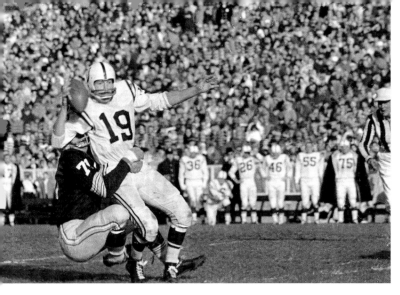

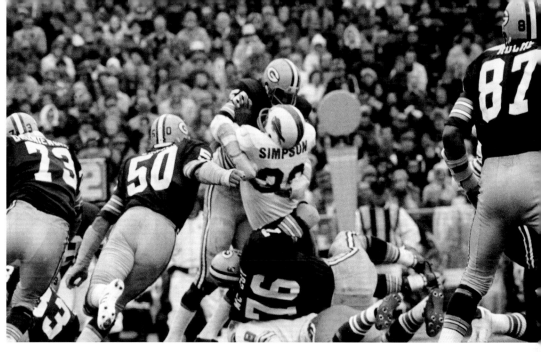

▲ Linebacker Bill Forester sacks Baltimore quarterback Johnny Unitas for an 11-yard loss during the second quarter of the Packers' 17-13 victory over the Colts on Nov. 18, 1962. Forester had four sacks in the game.

▲ Buffalo running back O.J. Simpson (32) is sandwiched by linebacker Ted Hendricks (56), on top, linebacker Jim Carter (50), in the middle, and defensive tackle Mike McCoy (76), on the bottom, during the Bills' 27-7 victory over the Packers on Oct. 6, 1974.

◄ Oakland Raiders coach John Madden looks on during his team's 28-3 victory over the Packers on Sept. 17, 1978. It was Madden's last season as a coach. He went into broadcasting in 1980 and returned to Lambeau Field — one of his favorite NFL stadiums — many times.

▲ Minnesota quarterback Fran Tarkenton (10) scrambles away from defensive tackle Dave Hanner (79) during the Packers' 24-23 loss to the Vikings on Oct. 4, 1964.

▲ Bears quarterback Jim McMahon, left, talks to coach Mike Ditka during Chicago's 16-10 victory over the Packers on Nov. 3, 1985.

▶ Chicago Bears coach Mike Ditka shouts at his team during its 25-12 victory over the Packers on Sept. 22, 1986.

▼ Bears running back Walter Payton (34) congratulates defensive tackle-turned-fullback William "The Refrigerator" Perry (72) after Perry scored a touchdown in Chicago's 25-12 victory over the Packers on Sept. 22, 1986.

▲ The Packers honor Chicago Bears running back Walter Payton before his last game at Lambeau Field on Nov. 8, 1987. Payton received a picture and a helmet from Judge Robert Parins, the Packers' president, and Scott Berchtold, right, of the Packers' public relations staff.

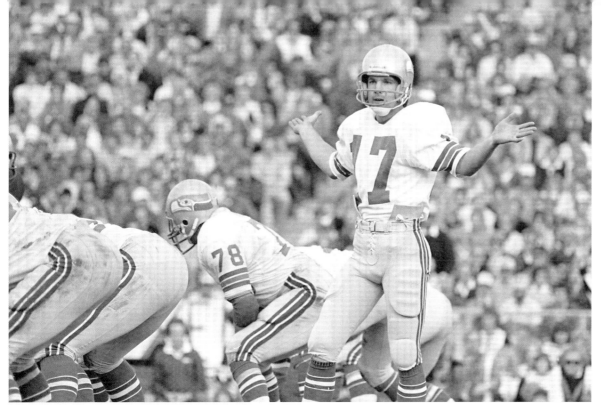

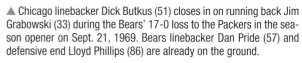

▲ Chicago linebacker Dick Butkus (51) closes in on running back Jim Grabowski (33) during the Bears' 17-0 loss to the Packers in the season opener on Sept. 21, 1969. Bears linebacker Dan Pride (57) and defensive end Lloyd Phillips (86) are already on the ground.

▼ Philadelphia defensive end Reggie White (92) is congratulated by his teammates after deflecting a pass by Packers quarterback Don Majkowski (7) during the Eagles' 20-3 victory on Sept. 1, 1991.

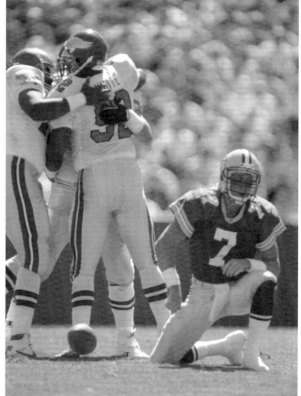

▲ Lambeau Field fans make so much noise for so long — almost 10 minutes — that Seattle quarterback Dave Krieg can't call his signals and is forced to plead for quiet during the fourth quarter of the Packers' 34-24 victory over the Seahawks on Nov. 1, 1981.

▶ Linebackers Brian Noble (91) and Johnny Holland (50) gang up on Los Angeles running back Marcus Allen during the Raiders' 20-0 victory over the Packers on Sept. 13, 1987.

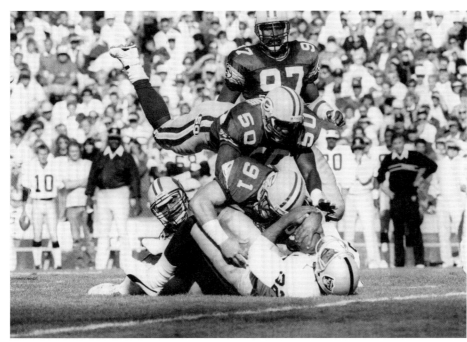

CHAPTER FIVE
THE STADIUM SCENE

Through the years, Lambeau Field has been a stage for colorful sights, sounds and characters.

Woven into the fabric of the historic stadium's mystique, some of these scenes and people have not been always visible to the Packers faithful on game day.

Since the beginning in 1957, when the facility was known as City Stadium, thousands of people have toiled in the shadow of football greats, contributing to legend and lore.

Sometimes they were people just doing their regular jobs. Sometimes they were volunteers staffing concession stands to raise money for their nonprofit organizations. Sometimes they were Green Bay-area residents working for one day on snow-removal crews in the northernmost completely uncovered stadium in the National Football League.

They've worked in virtually every nook and cranny of the fabled stadium. From the inner sanctums below the stadium bowl to the top level of the press box, they have always been essential to the Lambeau scene.

DRESSING ROOM PASS

GREEN BAY PACKERS
VS
PHILADELPHIA EAGLES
SUN., NOV. 25, 1979   LAMBEAU FIELD

GOOD FOR BOTH HOME AND VISITORS LOCKERS.
WORKING PERSONNEL ONLY PLEASE.
(No children or non-authorized personnel)

◄ Mark Brady, right, shovels snow onto a slide to get the seating area ready for the Packers' game against the Detroit Lions four days later, on Dec. 22, 1990.

► John Proski mows the playing field during the 1968 preseason.

▶ The bunting and Titletown U.S.A. banners are up along the railing and the tarp is rolled back as the finishing touches are applied to the south end zone at City Stadium on Dec. 29, 1961, two days before the NFL championship game between the Packers and New York Giants.

▲ Press-Gazette photographer Ken Behrend uses a telephoto lens to capture the action on the field from the press box during a 1961 game at City Stadium.

▲ Jack Orde paints the words "Green Bay" in the south end zone at City Stadium on Dec. 29, 1961.

▲ Arnold DesJardins stands in the knee-deep hay under the goal posts in the south end zone in early December 1961. The hay was put on the field to preserve it for a month before the NFL championship game.

▲ Steam rises from a kettle at a concession stand beneath City Stadium during the NFL championship game on Dec. 31, 1961.

◄A CBS camera points toward the field from the City Stadium press box during a 1963 game.

▼ Play-by-play man Ray Scott, left, and color analyst Tony Canadeo, far right, call a game for CBS during the 1963 season. They called all the Packers' regular-season games on TV for most of the 1960s. The man at center is unidentified.

◄▼ Halfback Paul Hornung runs up the 60 rows at City Stadium in April 1964 while preparing for his comeback from a year's suspension for gambling. Below, he sits on the ground, sweating.

▶ Trainer Bud Jorgensen wraps halfback Paul Hornung's right ankle before a workout in July 1964. It was Jorgensen's 41st year with the team. He retired in 1970.

▼ Press-Gazette writers Art Daley, center, and Lee Remmel work in the press box during the Packers' preseason game against the Pittsburgh Steelers on Aug. 27, 1966. Daley covered the Packers for the Press-Gazette from 1941 to 1968; Remmel did so from 1944 to 1974, when he joined the Packers as director of public relations. The press box was named for Remmel in 2003.

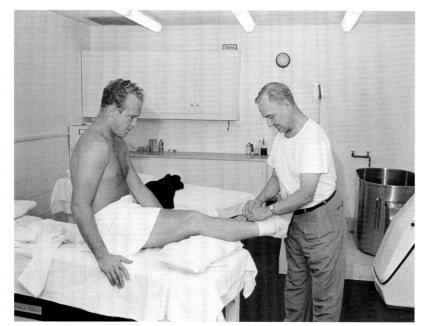

▲ A member of the City Stadium maintenance crew climbs a Green Bay Fire Department ladder to replace a light on one of the towers in August 1964. The tower rises 110 feet above the stadium.

▲ A worker sweeps snow from the seats before the home finale against the Detroit Lions on Dec. 3, 1972.

▲ The Packers check out a new weightlifting machine in July 1967. From left, defensive back Doug Hart (43), guard Gale Gillingham (68), linebacker Tommy Joe Crutcher (56), defensive back Herb Adderley (26) and tackle Forrest Gregg (75).

◄ This motivational sign was above the Packers' weight room, which was filled with members of the media when this photo was taken Sept. 21, 1982, as NFL players started a two-month strike.

▶ Film editor Al Treml stands in his library in May 1973.

▼ Bill Tobin, the Packers' director of professional scouting, scans a board full of players' names in his office in May 1973.

▲ The left portion of this sign, reading "It's Time," was taken off the Packers' locker room wall in December 1972, when they reached the playoffs for the first time in five years.

◀ Radio announcer Jim Irwin sets up for a broadcast before a 1976 game. Irwin started as an analyst on Packers broadcasts in 1969, then became the team's play-by-play voice in 1975, teaming first with former player Lionel Aldridge, then with former players Max McGee and Larry McCarren. Irwin retired after the 1998 season.

▲ Packers players listen to coach Forrest Gregg at a team meeting during the week before the season finale against the Minnesota Vikings in mid-December 1984.

▲ Clem Collard, 78, was the press box chief at Lambeau Field as the 1984 season began. He hadn't missed a Packers home game since 1920 — except for the first half of one game. "Back in 1922 or '23, I had a cold," he said.

◄ Equipment manager Bob Noel is framed by two racks of practice jerseys in the Packers' equipment room during training camp in 1985.

▲ From left, defensive linemen Blaise Winter, Lester Archambeau and Shawn Patterson sit together in the locker room as the players clean out their lockers a day after a 22-13 loss at Denver ended the Packers' 1990 season.

▲ This was the first group of fans to go through Lambeau Field when the Packers started conducting tours in June 1991. The tours are a popular attraction, but were halted while the stadium was renovated in 2002 and 2003.

▲ Bob Wozniak paints lines on the field before preseason play begins in August 1990.

◄ Cheng Chang, left, and other workers clear trash from the aisles after a September 1992 game.

▲ Workers roll out the tarp to try to keep the Lambeau Field sod from freezing in January 1995.

▲ Marge Switzer inspects left tackle John Michels' jersey before the Packers' game against the Minnesota Vikings in September 1997. She handles all uniform alterations and repairs, tailoring them to the players' requests.

◀ Packers fans lounge in the Lambeau Field club seats, watching the NFL draft on April 24, 1994.

▶ Crews paint the end zone in preparation for the NFC championship game against the Carolina Panthers on Jan. 12, 1997.

▼ Derek Paris of the Packers' grounds crew checks the temperature of the playing field on Jan. 3, 2003, a day before the playoff game against the Atlanta Falcons. He's making sure the ground hasn't frozen. The air temperature was 31 at kickoff the next day.

▲ With the Packers on the road for two weeks, crews remove the SportGrass playing surface in mid-October 1999. The hybrid surface of natural grass and synthetic turf proved troublesome from the time it was installed in 1997. First, the grass died. Then, the field got too sandy. Finally, in 1999, the field got too slippery and was replaced with natural grass after just five games.

▲ Nose tackle Gilbert Brown (93) and defensive end Reggie White (92) stand in the tunnel on the north end of the field, waiting to be introduced before the Packers' game against the Minnesota Vikings on Sept. 21, 1997.

▲ More than 300 people show up in single-digit temperatures to help clear 6 to 8 inches of snow from the stands at Lambeau Field on Dec. 20, 2000, four days before the Packers hosted the Tampa Bay Buccaneers. It took about five hours. Workers were paid $7 an hour.

CHAPTER SIX

GAME DAY

Hours before kickoff, the flags are hoisted. The charcoal fires are lit. The costumes are donned. The faces are painted. Game day at Lambeau Field is all about the Green Bay Packers and football, to be sure.

But game day is also about reveling in a festive atmosphere found only in Green Bay.

Some insist that tailgating before and after National Football League games started in the parking lot of Lambeau Field back in the late 1950s, when it was still known as City Stadium.

Beyond the tailgating, though, Lambeau Field stands alone by its location smack dab in a city neighborhood. Homeowners and businesses cash in on their proximity to the stadium by charging for lawn parking.

Creating a college-town atmosphere, restaurants and taverns put up tents, hire bands and invite fans to party. If you're not lucky enough to have a ticket, you can buy a beverage and watch the game on big screens within eyesight of the stadium and earshot of the roar when the Packers score.

The sights, sounds and smells of game day in the neighborhood around Lambeau Field, long before the Packers take the field, remain a unique experience in the world of professional sports.

◀ The wave arrives at Lambeau Field in 1985, going around the stadium during the fourth quarter of the Packers' 23-20 victory over the New York Giants in their home opener on Sept. 15. The phenomenon was so new that it was described as "a wave cheer."

▶ Packers fans from Iron Mountain, Mich., show their loyalty during the game against the Baltimore Colts on Sept. 29, 1963.

▲ A well-known Berlin store dressed a busload of Packers fans in furs for the NFL championship game on Dec. 31, 1961.

▲ A man stands atop a snow pile to get a better view of the field during the NFL championship game against the New York Giants on Dec. 31, 1961.

▶ The temperature was 20 at kickoff of the 1961 NFL championship game. But by the time the Packers had routed the New York Giants 37-0, the cold didn't matter to this fan, who went topless in celebration in the parking lot.

> *One of the things I've always said is that if you're a sports enthusiast there are four places you have to go to see a game. You should go to Notre Dame. You should go to Wrigley Field. You should go see a game at Fenway Park and you should go to Lambeau Field. I've been to all four, and Lambeau is No. 1 because more so than the places I just named there's just a feel to it the moment you drive up because it grabs a hold of you.*
>
> *"I'll never forget the Carolina game, which the Packers had to win to get to the first Super Bowl under Holmgren. As you sat in the stadium with four or five minutes left knowing the Packers were going to the Super Bowl in New Orleans, I never felt anything like it. It was spine-tingling. The postgame show usually lasted 15 minutes, but after 35 minutes the producers were telling us to get off the air. But Max (McGee), Larry (McCarren) and I didn't want to go anywhere else. We just wanted to stay there and soak in everything."*

— **Jim Irwin, Packers radio voice, 1969-98**

▲ Wisconsin Gov. Warren Knowles, smiling at center, sits with Green Bay broadcasting executive Ben Laird, wearing hat, during a game against the Minnesota Vikings on Dec. 5, 1965.

▲ The Packers' Golden Girls form the letter P in the south end zone before a game in 1965. The majorette at center is Susie Van Duyse; the majorette at right is Mary Jane Van Duyse. The rest of the group includes Nancy Bongle, Peggy Carstens, Marcie DeNamur, Maribeth Hartwig, Kathy Keefe, Janet Krieser, Lynette Kurtz, Kathy Laundrie, Jodie Londo, Cheryl Mueller, Susie Nelson, Nancy Notz, Sandy Parmentier, Shirley Remick, Terry Sant Amour, Lynda Schopf, Sally Spaid, Mary Stiller, Pattie Tilden and Dana Weckler.

▲ Packers cheerleaders warm up on the sidelines during the season opener against the Detroit Lions on Sept. 20, 1970. Choreographer Shirley Van is at left.

◀ Mary Jane Van Duyse, the Packers' Golden Girl, twirls flaming batons at halftime of the Packers' preseason game against the New York Giants on Aug. 14, 1965.

" Lambeau Field to me is the Mecca of pro football. Anybody who is a true football fan should have the experience of going there at least one time. It's a marvelous place. I don't think there's any place at any level of football that equals Lambeau Field."

— Ron Wolf, Packers general manager, 1991-2001

▶ Not quite dressed for 10-degree weather, some of the Packers' cheerleaders try to stay warm in front of a sideline heater during the home finale against the Detroit Lions on Dec. 3, 1972.

▼ Between her muffler and his pipe, Mae and Henry Pahlow stay warm during the home finale on Dec. 3, 1972.

▲ Wilner Burke directs the Packer Band before the game against the Oakland Raiders on Sept. 17, 1978. Tracing its roots to old City Stadium as the Packer Lumberjack Band, the group was a familiar sight — and sound — before and during games through the 1996 season.

▲ The temperature was just 6 degrees at kickoff of the Packers' home finale against the Chicago Bears on Nov. 28, 1976. It didn't seem to bother this fan, who warded off the cold with a bottle of peppermint schnapps.

▲ A vendor carries a case of beer and a stack of cups through the Lambeau Field stands during the Packers' home opener against the Houston Oilers on Sept. 25, 1977.

▲ Brightly painted fans are nothing new at Lambeau Field. Blaine Walesh of Two Rivers, then 21, painted his head and face as a green-and-gold Packers helmet for a preseason game in August 1983.

▲ A thirsty fan tries to coax just one more beer from a concession stand during a preseason game against the Philadelphia Eagles on Aug. 20, 1983. The stand ran out of beer before halftime, and no beer was sold in the stands.

▲ Brian Hestrich of Sheboygan and Lisa Peterson of Sturgeon Bay wear green and gold grass skirts as they tailgate before a preseason game in August 1983.

◄ Coach Bart Starr's Packers are 2-6 when they host Seattle on Nov. 1, 1981. Some fans aren't happy, including these tailgaters, some of whom wanted to "bag Bart." The Packers beat the Seahawks 34-24 and won six of their last eight games to finish 8-8.

▲ Stephanie Infante, right, the wife of coach Lindy Infante, reacts to a play as she and others watch the Packers' 1991 opener against the Philadelphia Eagles from a skybox. The Packers lost 20-3.

▲ Some fans didn't hide their disappointment about the Packers' 1-5 start in 1991, as seen during a 10-0 loss to the Chicago Bears on Oct. 17, 1991.

▶ Wisconsin Gov. Tommy Thompson, left, shakes the hand of Nancy Ellis, the sister of President George H.W. Bush and the aunt of future President George W. Bush, as they campaign outside Lambeau Field on Oct. 25, 1992.

▲ At top, a member of the Burlington High School marching band wears mittens while playing a flute at halftime of the Packers' game against the Detroit Lions on Dec. 15, 1991. It was 10 degrees at kickoff. Fans leave little to chance — and little skin exposed — during the game.

▼ Packers fans will do almost anything to bring their team luck, including bringing a troll doll, as did Butch Homewood of Green Bay and Delores Vogels of De Pere at a preseason game against the New England Patriots on Aug. 26, 1994.

▲ Fans seeking tickets often walk through the Lambeau Field parking lot, as this man did before a 1996 game.

▼ Some Packers fans are as recognizable as the players, including Larry Primeau of De Pere (the Packalope) and Bob Wagner of Oshkosh (Gang Green), seen during a 1996 game.

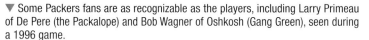

▲ John O'Neill of Madison started attending Packers games in 1964, but didn't start dressing as St. Vince until he attended Super Bowl XXXI in January 1997. Here, he cheers at the Packers' season opener against the Chicago Bears on Sept. 1, 1997.

◄ Erin Rahn of Milwaukee wears her game face during the 1996 season.

◄ The foam cheesehead has become a popular piece of game-day attire, as demonstrated at a 1996 game.

▶ Parking lot attendant Henry Francois, right, directs a customer before the Packers' game against the Minnesota Vikings on Sept. 21, 1997. Francois started that job when new City Stadium opened in 1957.

▼ Al Hale pours a beer during the Packers' game on Sept. 21, 1997 He's always worked in Sections 17 and 19, near the 50-yard line. When he started in 1963, beer was 35 cents a bottle, or three for $1.

▲ Lambeau Field has long been a favorite destination for fans, and a favorite backdrop for their photos. Mike Planey of South Bend, Ind., takes a photograph of his wife, Sandi, left, and friends Mike and Judy Fedore as they visit during training camp in August 1999.

> " I've talked to people all over the world, and for a sports fan going to Lambeau is like a pilgrimage to Mecca. It used to be Yankee Stadium, and I think maybe it still is for a number of baseball fans. But Lambeau Field has become the one spot for people to see before they die if they're football fans.
>
> "I think of the wonderful memories, the friendships, the battles fought. When I get close to Lambeau my heart beats a little faster because I can't wait to see it. My whole system kind of picks up a notch or two. I remember all of the moments with Coach Lombardi and all the guys. It's a wonderful series of memories that comes back."
>
> — *Jerry Kramer, Packers guard, 1958-68*

◄ The parking lot on the east side of Lambeau Field is filled with fans and tailgaters before the Packers' game against the Philadelphia Eagles on Sept. 17, 2000.

▼ As if their body paint and headbands didn't say it all, these Packers fans chant "Go, Pack, go!" during a preseason game against the Cleveland Browns on Aug. 26, 2002.

▲ As work on the Lambeau Field renovation continues, fans wait to go through security checkpoints at the temporary north gate before the Packers' playoff game against the San Francisco 49ers on Jan. 13, 2002.

TAILGATING

Packers flags fly above the rows of vehicles crammed into the Lambeau Field lot. Cheesehead-topped fans mill around parking lots, tending to grills and mixing drinks. A potpourri of smells — burning charcoal and grilling hamburgers, hot dogs and brats — wafts over the crowd. There's beer and booze and Bloody Marys in the making.

Green Bay Packers fans are rarely shy about their love for all things green and gold, but that passion takes on a fevered pitch on game day. Beads, wigs, clown shoes, ties, hats, cars, tents, grills, tables and chairs all can be found in Packers colors.

The party didn't start with such intensity.

For Packers fans, tailgating started out of necessity.

When the new City Stadium opened in 1957, it was surrounded by farm fields. Out-of-town ticket holders could find no place to grab a meal when they arrived for games. Fans would bring a hot dish or sandwiches in the car and eat a quick lunch in the parking lot. Later, when portable grills hit the market, people started to cook out at Lambeau.

Tailgating grows more sophisticated by the season, making game day an all-out event. Gas and charcoal grills, gas-powered blenders and smokers all can be

▼ The air is filled with smoke from charcoal grills and the aroma of grilled food in the Lambeau Field parking lot before the game against the Chicago Bears on Dec. 13, 1998.

found turning out feasts.

Of course, Green Bay doesn't hold the honor of being the only place where tailgating is taken almost as seriously as the game itself, but fans here have received some national recognition.

Tailgating.com named Green Bay as one of the three best places to tailgate in the professional football category in its 2002-03 State of Tailgating report. Kansas City and Buffalo, N.Y., also were recognized as great venues to tailgate.

The site says this about tailgating, Packers style: "Legendary, surreal, magical and the best brats."

▲ The Packer Picnic Club tailgates before the Sept. 13, 1964, opener against the Chicago Bears. From left, are George and Betsy Yonan of Chicago and Mr. and Mrs. James Kimberly, formerly of Neenah. The club, made up largely of prominent people from Appleton, Neenah and Menasha, had rented tailgating space for 65 cars across from City Stadium since its opening in 1957.

◀ From left, Col. John Sensenbrenner of Neenah, Trudy Sensenbrenner of Appleton and her grandfather, J. Leslie Sensenbrenner of Neenah, look on as the Packer Picnic Club sets up its tailgate party before the Sept. 13, 1964, opener against the Bears.

▲ Packers fans come from throughout Wisconsin, and many of them enjoy tailgating. This group of 19, from Hurley, made its annual trip to a preseason game on Aug. 30, 1980. Their tailgate party started at 9:30 a.m. for a night game against the Denver Broncos.

▲ Steve Sorenson of Pittsfield watches as John Hilbert of Howard bastes lobster at a tailgate party before the game against the Chicago Bears on Oct. 17, 1991.

▶ Sometimes, fans don't even need a home game. These seven men were part of a group of 25 people who tailgated and watched the Packers' 1981 season finale — a 28-3 loss to the New York Jets at Shea Stadium — on TV in the Lambeau Field parking lot on Dec. 20. From left are Dave Michaud, Bruce Hansen, Jim Hansen, Dave Thelen, Woody Glime, Bob Simons and Paul Gagnon. They'd done so since 1978 because the Packers finished on the road in each of those seasons.

◀ A Christmas tree at her side, Sue Primeau of De Pere makes sandwiches while tailgating before the Packers' game against the Denver Broncos on Dec. 8, 1996.

▼ Fans come from throughout Wisconsin to tailgate before games. This group plays a game of cards before heading into the stadium for the Packers' game against the Minnesota Vikings on Sept. 21, 1997. Clockwise from lower left at the table: Bob and Audrey Janke of Baraboo and Don and Ardys Janke of Ripon.

“ Green Bay, Wisconsin, population 102,313, has a football stadium seating more than 72,000. Yes. Lambeau Field, home of the Green Bay Packers, is a unique place indeed. Plus, it now ranks among the five most famous locations in sports history along with Yankee Stadium of New York, Soldier Field of Chicago, Fenway Park of Boston and Wrigley Field of Chicago.

"Lambeau Field came into its own when the Packers ended a 42-year partnership with Milwaukee (County Stadium) after the 1994 season. Now it's a 'Monday Night Football' fixture even though Green Bay has no skyline like its other four partners."

— **Art Daley, former Green Bay Press-Gazette sports editor**

▲ Carol Wilson of De Pere tosses steaks onto a grill as she and friends tailgate before the Packers' season opener against the Los Angeles Raiders on Sept. 13, 1987.

CHAPTER SEVEN

THE NEW LAMBEAU

At the dawn of the 21st century, the Green Bay Packers remained a throwback to simpler times, still the only publicly owned franchise in professional sports, flourishing in a small Midwestern city.

But in the face of the harsh financial realities of modern pro football, it was going to take more than legend and lore to keep the Packers economically viable into the future.

Enter Bob Harlan, the Packers' president and chief executive officer. His plan to help the team generate revenue revolved literally and figuratively around the hallowed ground of Lambeau Field.

In the National Football League, teams share earnings from tickets, television and merchandise sold around the country. But they can keep money earned from concessions, parking and merchandise sold at their stadiums. By building a modern atrium for special events, suitable for year-round use, the Packers would have a steady revenue stream.

Other NFL teams have turned to modern structures to generate more revenue, and the Packers also considered building new. But in e-mails and conversations, fans made clear to Harlan that they wanted to save Lambeau Field.

The first hurdle was structural. Could the

stadium, opened in 1957, support the renovations needed to extend its life and bring in more revenue? Yes it could, the engineers said.

The next hurdle: the $295 million price tag.

The Packers had no choice but to turn again to the fans and the community that had supported them since 1919.

They had asked for fans' financial support for Lambeau Field renovations as early as November 1997, conducting the fourth stock sale in the team's history, raising more than $24 million for capital improvements.

Then in 2000, fans were asked to contribute a one-time $2,000-a-seat user fee — $1,400 from Green package ticket holders and $600 from Gold package ticket holders, many of the latter former Milwaukee ticket holders.

Residents of Brown County were asked to pick up the biggest part of the tab by approving a 0.5 percent county sales tax. An intense community debate ensued. The Packers are a source of fierce hometown pride for the Green Bay area, but a new tax is never a popular topic.

In the weeks leading up to the referendum, Harlan and John Jones, the Packers' executive vice president and chief operating

The steel framework of the new Lambeau Field is lit up at night in late January 2002. Construction crews worked night and day on the project.

Bumper sticker from Lambeau Field renovation campaign, 2000.

officer, spoke at dozens of community gatherings to explain the project.

On Sept. 12, 2000, Brown County voters approved the sales-tax referendum, 48,788 to 42,580, or 53 percent to 47 percent.

The Packers, the city of Green Bay, the NFL and season-ticket holders contributed $125.9 million toward the renovation. Bonding supported by the 0.5 percent Brown County sales tax provided $160 million. The state of Wisconsin paid $9.1 million for stadium infrastructure improvements.

Also in place was a plan that would allow the city of Green Bay to defray some of the public cost by selling the naming rights to Lambeau Field.

On Jan. 3, 2001, the new Green Bay-Brown County Professional Stadium District approved a lease agreement with the Packers, who will have access to the facility until 2033.

At a victory celebration on the night of the vote, Harlan addressed a crowd of jubilant supporters.

"The whole country tonight is watching Green Bay, Wisconsin," Harlan said. "And as it has so many times in the past, this team and this community have gotten together to perform one more miracle."

▼ As the sun rises over Lambeau Field on game day, there's already plenty going on in and around the stadium. This photo was taken on the morning of Sept. 21, 1997, before the Packers played the Minnesota Vikings.

Lambeau Field timeline

1955: After having had to listen to other NFL teams grumble about old City Stadium, the Packer Corporation tells Green Bay City Council that it wants a new stadium.

1956: By a margin of 11,575 to 4,893, Green Bay voters approve a $960,000 bond issue on April 3. Green Bay architect John E. Somerville is hired to design a new city stadium. The cost of the stadium, to be built by Geo. M. Hougard & Sons of Green Bay, is shared by the city and the Packers.

1957: New City Stadium, with a capacity of 32,150, is dedicated on Sept. 29. Vice President Richard Nixon attends the game. The Packers beat the Bears 21-17. Surprisingly, there are 18 no-shows. Packers average 26,850 per home game in three Green Bay games and three Milwaukee games.

1960: Let the waiting list begin! All season tickets are sold out for the first time and have been ever since. More than 200,000 people see the Packers play at home for the first time. The team responds by winning the Western Conference championship.

1961: The first Vince Lombardi-era NFL title. Stadium capacity is increased to 38,669.

1963: The Packers add 3,658 seats to capacity, bringing total to 42,327. More than 300,000 people attend Packers home games in Green Bay and Milwaukee.

1965: E.L. "Curly" Lambeau dies in Sturgeon Bay on June 1. City Stadium is rededicated as Lambeau Field on Sept. 11. Seating capacity is increased to 50,852.

▲ The east side of Lambeau Field, seen during the 1997 season.

1967: Heating coils are first installed under the playing surface, but they fail to work on Dec. 31 as the Packers defeat the Dallas Cowboys 21-17 in the Ice Bowl, the coldest recorded game in NFL history. Though official seating capacity is 50,852, official attendance is announced at 50,861.

1970: The bowl around the stadium becomes complete; capacity is increased to 56,263.

1978: The city of Green Bay becomes the owner of Lambeau Field as the original mortgage is paid off. The Packers pass 400,000 in home attendance for the first time.

1982: Packers are beaten by Detroit Lions 30-10 on Dec. 12. It is the only regular-season game at Lambeau Field that season because of the NFL players' strike.

1985: Private boxes — 72 of them — are added to Lambeau Field by Jacob C. Basten Construction Co. of Green Bay. Most boxes are on the east side; a few are on the west side, flanking the press box. Capacity increases

> " I think Lambeau Field, in many ways, is a symbol of what football in America is all about. It is open air. It is tradition. It includes not just Vince Lombardi, it includes Curly Lambeau, it includes the entire nine decades of the history of the National Football League."
>
> — *Paul Tagliabue,*
> *NFL commissioner*

to 56,926. The Selmer Co. of Green Bay builds the press-box addition.

1990: Capacity is increased to 59,543 with the addition of 36 luxury boxes and 1,920 club seats in the south end zone.

1993: The Lambeau Leap is born when safety LeRoy Butler tries jumping into the stands after returning a lateral for a touchdown in a December game against the Los Angeles Raiders. The first of Lambeau Field's ultimate big-screen TVs — a $1.7 million Sony JumboTron color replay board — is installed in the north end zone.

1994: Lambeau Field is adorned with the names of Packers in the Pro Football Hall of Fame and the dates of the Packers' NFL championships.

▶ On Dec. 24, 2000, the Packers hosted the Tampa Bay Buccaneers in the last game before the $295 million stadium renovation project begins. It was 15 degrees at kickoff, with subzero wind chills.

▼ Trying to convince Brown County voters of the need for a 0.5 percent sales tax to pay for a $295 million renovation project, the Packers welcome visitors for a tour of Lambeau Field on July 22, 2000.

1995: The Lambeau Leap is raised to an art form by Robert Brooks on Sept. 17, during a 14-6 win over the New York Giants. The Milwaukee portion of the movable football feast ends. For the first time since 1933, the Packers play all their home games in Green Bay. Capacity increases to 60,890 with the addition of 90 private boxes and an auxiliary press box. New $210,000 sound system is installed.

1996: With a price tag more than three times what it cost originally to build the stadium in 1957, new scoreboards are added for $3.5 million.

1997: New $1 million playing surface is installed. It includes heating, drainage and irrigation systems.

1998: The Packers raise more than $24 million in a stock sale and commit the proceeds to improvements to Lambeau Field and player training facilities. Packers executives meet with architects to determine what renovations can be made to the aging stadium.

1999: The team puts on hold a major renovation of Lambeau Field, saying it can't afford it, given the rising cost of staying competitive. Packers President

Bob Harlan says a new stadium may be needed within a decade. Fans press for another look at renovation.

2000: Harlan announces plan to renovate Lambeau Field for $295 million, funded largely by a 0.5 percent Brown County sales tax and a seat license fee paid by season-ticket holders. An atrium would be built to accommodate year-round use of the facility. On Sept. 12, Brown County voters pass the sales tax, 53 percent to 47 percent.

2001: Work on the renovation begins in January, but the official groundbreaking is delayed until May 19 in deference to warmer weather. As part of the ceremonies, 872 people form a semi-circle from the south end zone to the 50-yard line for a group hug, coming just short of a world record for group-hug participants but raising almost $30,000 for Special Olympics.

2002: The preseason welcomes fans to a new-look Lambeau Field. The luxury boxes are finished, the upper and lower concourses are open except on the north end and the Atrium forms a new main entrance to the

stadium, although many of the Atrium's amenities will await the 2003 season.

2003: The fully renovated Lambeau Field hosts its first regular-season game on Sept. 7, against the Minnesota Vikings.

▲ Ground is broken for the Lambeau Field renovation project on May 19, 2001, by having team representatives, politicians and guests dig into a sand sculpture rather than dig up the playing field.

▲ Steel lettering that once read "Green Bay Packers" lies in the north end zone at Lambeau Field as renovation work continues on Jan. 30, 2002.

▲ The old exterior wall on the east side of Lambeau Field is visible as iron workers erect the steel framework for the new Atrium and team offices in late October 2001.

RECONSTRUCTING LAMBEAU FIELD

March 1, 2001

April 16, 2001

May 16, 2001

October 18, 2001

November 9, 2001

December 7, 2001

May 14, 2002

June 26, 2002

July 12, 2002

January 2, 2003

January 30, 2003

February 19, 2003

Rebuilding a legendary stadium isn't cheap, about $295 million, nor does the work get done overnight. Here's a look at some of the work that went into reconstructing a legend.

July 31, 2001

August 14, 2001

September 14, 2001

January 8, 2002

February 12, 2002

April 9, 2002

September 10, 2002

December 11, 2002

December 26, 2002

March 14, 2003

March 26, 2003

April 18, 2003

BEHIND THE SCENES

▲ The office of Bob Harlan, the Packers' president and chief executive officer, is on the club level. It overlooks the Packers' practice fields to the east.

◀ Center Mike Flanagan, left, and left guard Mike Wahle play cards in the Packers' new locker room.

▼ Defensive coordinator Ed Donatell's office sits high above the Lambeau Field Atrium on the upper concourse level.

▲ Visitors to the Packers' offices make their first stop in the lobby on the upper concourse level, where LaFawn Joslin works at the desk.

◀ Historic photos are used throughout the concourse areas to lend a classic feel to the renovated stadium.

Championship - Packers fans in New York

▲ The Packers' locker room is at the heart of the players' work area. The hallways off the locker room lead to workout and treatment areas, to meeting and interview rooms and to the players' lounge.

▲ Right guard Marco Rivera is interviewed by a television crew at his locker.

▲ Linebacker Nick Barnett (56) is among the Packers enjoying the players' lounge. Television, video games and Internet access are available in the lounge, which is just off the locker room.

▶ As they gather in their position meeting room, the Packers' running backs are surrounded by photos of the team's legends at the rear, and by photos of more contemporary players along the side.

▲ Quarterback Brett Favre's locker.

◀ The Packers walk under this inspirational banner as they leave their locker room to head across the parking lot to the practice facilities.

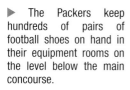

▶ The Packers keep hundreds of pairs of football shoes on hand in their equipment rooms on the level below the main concourse.

▼ The Packers' helmets and other gear are stored in equipment rooms.

◀▲ There's a basketball court with a parquet floor for the Packers' use on the level below the main concourse. Adjacent to it are two racquetball courts.

◀ The Packers have both a conventional whirlpool and a SwimEx rehabilitation pool just off their locker room. The SwimEx pool allows players to run or walk against an adjustable current. It also has an underwater observation deck, allowing the Packers' training staff to monitor a player's progress.

▼ The Packers' players often start their day in the training room, which is just off the locker room. There, they receive treatment and get their ankles taped.

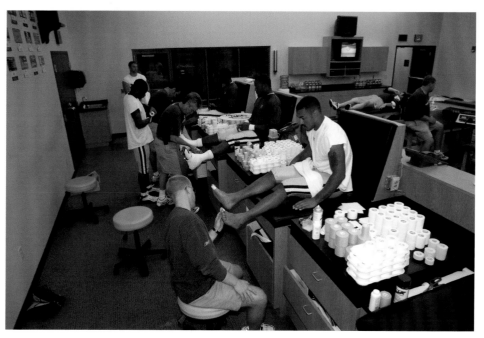

▲ Defensive backs coach Bob Slowik, right, works with his players in their meeting room. At the rear are large photos of Bobby Dillon, Willie Wood, Herb Adderley and LeRoy Butler, four of the best defensive backs in Packers history.

◀ Visiting teams enter Lambeau Field from this narrow tunnel behind the goal posts in the south end zone.

▶ Only the referee and game officials are allowed in this dressing room on the main concourse level at the south end of the field.

▶ As the Packers run onto Lambeau Field from this tunnel in the southeast corner of the field, they cross three concrete blocks laid into the floor and surrounded by bricks. The three blocks come from the Packers' original entry tunnel on the north end of the field. Coach Mike Sherman asked that the blocks be preserved during renovation and made part of the new entry tunnel. An inspirational plaque was added to the wall at right; it reads "Proud generations of Green Bay Packers players, World Champions a record 12 times, have run over this very concrete to Greatness."

▲ The entrance to Lambeau Field's service floor — the level below the main concourse — has room enough for semi trucks. More often, there are any number of smaller vehicles in use.

▲ The football field on the terrazzo floor of the Lambeau Field Atrium is covered by tables near the food court. The 50-yard field is oriented to line up with the north end of the actual playing field. When you stand on the 10-yard line in the Atrium, you're even with the 10-yard line on the field.

▼ The glass front of the Lambeau Field Atrium, as seen from inside.

▲ The expanded press box, with room for more than 250 people, towers high above the seating bowl on the west side of the stadium. Coaches and broadcasters sit closest to the 50-yard line. Other media members sit from the 50-yard line to the south end zone.

▲ Banners commemorating the Packers' world championships hang in the hallway between the team's locker room and weight room.

▶ The luxury suites feature theater-style seating.

▼ There's plenty of room for fans to gather in the lounge on the club level on the east side of the stadium. The area is open to fans with club seats or luxury boxes.

▲ Another view of the lounge on the club level on the east side of the stadium. The doors in the background lead to the Lambeau Legends Club, a banquet area and ballroom. The Legends Club can be divided into up to four separate rooms for meetings and smaller gatherings.

◄ The Packers Pro Shop, just outside the entrance to the Lambeau Field Atrium, offers an extensive selection of clothing and souvenir items. It's a model for other NFL teams' retailing efforts. There's also a Game Day Pro Shop on the west side of the stadium.

▼ A server sets tables in the Lambeau Legends Club on the club level on the east side of the stadium. The hall can be subdivided into as many as four rooms for a wide variety of gatherings.

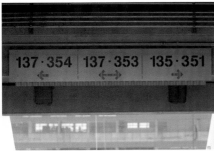

▲ ▶ Some reminders of the old Lambeau Field remain, such as the stenciled numbers directing fans to their sections.

PACKERS HALL OF FAME

For years, it has been the most visited hall of fame anywhere devoted to a single professional sports franchise.

Now that the Green Bay Packers Hall of Fame is in the Lambeau Field Atrium, it has more space — 25,000 square feet — for displays and interactive exhibits.

The sweeping, curved walls of the new Hall of Fame, in the lower level of the Atrium, usher fans through exhibits on the legends of yesterday and the stars of today.

Visitors start with an introductory film before heading off on a self-guided tour with a heavy emphasis on the interactive. The goal is that visitors learn something from their experience.

Theaters, exhibits and displays look at the stadium, fans and community and honor the greatest players ever to wear the green and gold. Hundreds of rare Packers-related artifacts date to the earliest days of professional football in Green Bay.

The Hall of Fame inducted its first class in 1970 and moved into its old building, across South Oneida Street, in 1975. Attendance slowly grew, then soared in

▼ This exhibit celebrates the training camp tradition of Packers players riding kids' bikes to practice. From left are plaster replicas of Kabeer Gbaja-Biamila and Donald Driver riding solo and Gilbert Brown with a passenger, all against a backdrop of the old exterior of Lambeau Field.

the Super Bowl years of the mid-1990s. In 1997, the Hall of Fame drew a record 259,019 visitors.

In its new setting, longtime popular exhibits have been combined with new attractions. Visitors can become part of life-size dioramas, such as one from the goal line of the Ice Bowl, that give fans a different way to look at the Packers and their stadium.

Some visitors spend hours perusing exhibits such as a timeline of champions, a 50-yard-line view, the locker room for Packers NFL Hall of Famers, the hall of inductees, the Packers' Super Bowl trophies and a Packers theater.

On the level above the Packers Pro Shop is an 8,000-square-foot interactive area. This space features a component designed with the assistance of educators from the Green Bay School District.

Popular with kids who get a chance to burn off steam, this level contains several high-energy skill games and interactive exhibits. Interactive categories — scouting, strategy and training — include information on how Vince Lombardi prepared his teams for each season.

▲ Pins, posters and Packers beads make up just part of the collection on display at the new Hall of Fame.

▲ A replica of coach Vince Lombardi's office is among the exhibits.

▼ This theater at the entrance to the new Hall of Fame offers repeated showings of a film detailing the Packers' rich history.

▲ At right, items from the Packers' training rooms are on display at the new Hall of Fame.

CHAPTER EIGHT

REDEDICATION: A NEW ERA BEGINS

On Sept. 7, 2003, the Green Bay Packers turned from their past to the future when the time came to rededicate "the best football stadium in the world — Lambeau Field."

Cory Jansa and Lacey Van Zeeland, two eighth-graders from Lombardi Middle School in Green Bay, took turns reading a short script during a halftime ceremony at midfield.

Their joint statement rededicated Lambeau Field "on behalf of all past, present and future generations of Packers fans from around the world," signaling the beginning of a new era for the longest continuously used pro football stadium in the country.

National Football League Commissioner Paul Tagliabue told the crowd, "The NFL would not be what it is today without the Green Bay Packers."

The brief rededication ceremony capped a weeklong series of special events. On the previous Sunday, more than 33,000 fans flocked to a free open house. The Robert E. Harlan Plaza, in front of the Atrium, was dedicated in honor of the Packers' president and chief executive officer. Former quarterback and coach Bart Starr and former general manager Ron Wolf joined in the dedication of the new Green Bay Packers Hall of Fame.

At a glittering gala in the Atrium, Harlan and his wife, Madeline, hosted a formal benefit that raised $450,000 for St. Mary's Hospital Medical Center. And 34,000 fans partied at a "Rebirth of a Legend" show paying tribute to the stadium and Packers legends from the earliest days of the franchise, through the Glory Years, to the present.

Outside the Atrium, the hoopla was presided over by the bronze images of the two most legendary figures in Packers history: Curly Lambeau and Vince Lombardi. The statues immediately became a magnet for camera-pointing fans.

◄ Lacey Van Zeeland, left, and Cory Jansa stand at the 50-yard line and address the crowd at the Lambeau Field rededication ceremony during halftime of the Packers' game against the Minnesota Vikings on Sept. 7, 2003. The eighth-graders from Lombardi Middle School in Green Bay were chosen as speakers after writing prize-winning Packers-related essays. Behind them, from left, are Packers treasurer John Underwood; Packers secretary Peter Platten; Packers vice president John Fabry; state Rep. John Gard; U.S. Rep. Mark Green; Wisconsin Gov. Jim Doyle; John Jones, the Packers' executive vice president and chief operating officer; and NFL commissioner Paul Tagliabue.

► A ticket from the first regular-season game at the renovated Lambeau Field is protected in a plastic sleeve attached to a lanyard.

Standing in their shadow, John Jones, the Packers' executive vice president and chief operating officer, spoke of the true significance of the renovation of Lambeau Field, a national treasure rooted in the team's history and reborn to secure its financial future.

"The Packers will be here in Green Bay for our children and our grandchildren," Jones said, "just as they were here for our parents and grandparents."

▲ The red carpet is rolled out for Packers quarterback Brett Favre and his wife, Deanna, center, as they arrive at the Lambeau Field inaugural ball on Sept. 5, 2003.

◄ Packers president and CEO Bob Harlan, center, is flanked by his son, Michael, and wife, Madeline, at left, and by his sons, Bryan and Kevin at right, as they unveil a plaque during the dedication ceremony for the Robert E. Harlan Plaza outside the stadium on Sept. 2, 2003.

▲ Guests walk up the stairs at the Oneida Nation Gate as they arrive at the Lambeau Field inaugural ball on Sept. 5, 2003.

◀ The Lambeau Field Atrium floor is covered with tables set for the inaugural ball.

▲ Ta-Koma King, 5, of Green Bay, dressed as a grass dancer, waits for his turn to perform with an Oneida Nation group at a Labor Day picnic at Lambeau Field on Sept. 1, 2003.

▶ Green Bay Police Capt. Ken Brodhagen, left, gives Packers trading cards to Ashlyn Fitzgerald, 3, of Allouez, at the Labor Day picnic. Men and women who were instrumental in building the renovated Lambeau Field were honored at the event.

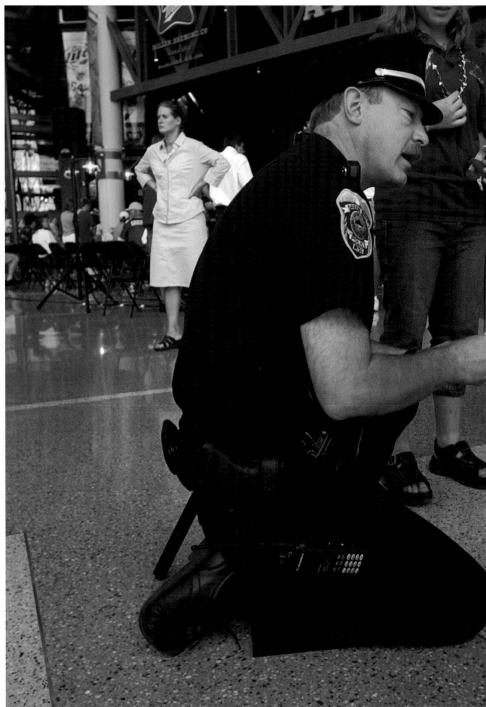

▲ Visitors to the new Packers Hall of Fame at Lambeau Field are silhouetted against displays detailing the team's more recent history.

◀ Packers legend Bart Starr, right, signs an autograph for Wendy Smetana of Green Bay, center, after the dedication of the new Packers Hall of Fame on Sept. 4, 2003.

▲ Packers greats Paul Hornung, Bart Starr and Jim Taylor walk onto the field after being introduced at the Rebirth of a Legend celebration at Lambeau Field on Sept. 6, 2003.

From left, Packers greats Paul Hornung, Jim Taylor and Bart Starr stand on the field after being introduced at the Rebirth of a Legend celebration. Above them, ringing the stadium bowl, are their names and the years they played for the Packers, an honor traditionally bestowed upon former Packers players inducted into the Pro Football Hall of Fame in Canton, Ohio.

Judy Russell of Oshkosh shows she was at the dedication of new City Stadium in 1957 as she watches the Rebirth of a Legend festivities.

The Rebirth of a Legend celebration, which offered an open house and entertainment, drew 33,899 people to Lambeau Field.

▲ Though much has changed at the renovated Lambeau Field, the recipe for tailgating remains the same — friends, food, refreshments, football and fun.

◄ Brad Moeller of Milwaukee carries his son, Brady, 3, to their seats before the Packers' preseason opener against the Carolina Panthers on Aug. 23, 2003.

◀ The bronze statue of Vince Lombardi towers over visitors to the Robert E. Harlan Plaza outside Lambeau Field.

▼ Randy Redman, right, points out the sights in the Lambeau Field Atrium to his children, Ryan, left, and Jordan, center, before the preseason game against Carolina on Aug. 23, 2003. Redman, his wife, Linda, and their children live in Woodstock, Ill., and are season-ticket holders.

▲ Fans walk along Packer Drive toward Lambeau Field before the Packers' preseason game against the Carolina Panthers on Aug. 23, 2003.

▲ Fans walk through the Lambeau Field Atrium before the Packers' season opener against the Minnesota Vikings on Sept. 7, 2003.

▶ Fans walk up new ramps to reach their seats before the Packers' preseason opener against the Carolina Panthers on Aug. 23, 2003.

▲ An oversized Packers logo is just one of the signature pieces of décor at Curly's Pub, a tavern and restaurant on the second level of the Lambeau Field Atrium.

▶ The Lambeau Field Atrium becomes the front door to Lambeau Field before the Packers' season opener against the Minnesota Vikings on Sept. 7, 2003.

▲ Keeping alive the tradition of live music at Packers game, this group performs in the Lambeau Field parking lot before the season opener against the Minnesota Vikings on Sept. 7, 2003. From left are Dave Sullivan on banjo, Andy Zipperer on trombone and Kurt Risch on drums.

◄ Paul Coffman, left, and John Anderson are among the former Green Bay players watching from the sidelines as the Packers take on the Vikings on opening day.

▲ Tailgaters fill the east parking lot at Lambeau Field before the season opener.

▲ Aaron Trotzer of Rothschild shows his true colors at the season opener against the Vikings.

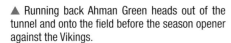

▲ Running back Ahman Green heads out of the tunnel and onto the field before the season opener against the Vikings.

▶ Cheerleaders lead the Packers onto the field before the season opener. From left, the players are Gilbert Brown (93), Josh Bidwell (9), Grey Ruegamer (67), Cletidus Hunt (97), Rob Davis (60) and Ryan Longwell (8).

▲ Fans lean on the roof of the tunnel leading from the Packers' locker room to the playing field as the teams warm up for the season opener between the Packers and Minnesota Vikings on Sept. 7, 2003.

▲ NFL commissioner Paul Tagliabue waves to fans during the Lambeau Field rededication ceremonies at halftime of the Packers' season opener against the Minnesota Vikings on Sept. 7, 2003. Behind him, from left, are Packers treasurer John Underwood; Packers secretary Peter Platten; Packers vice president John Fabry; state Rep. John Gard; U.S. Rep. Mark Green; Wisconsin Gov. Jim Doyle; Lombardi Middle School student Lacey Van Zeeland; John Jones, the Packers' executive vice president and chief operating officer; Lombardi Middle School student Cory Jansa; Donald Harden and Jim Temp, members of the Packers' executive committee; and Bob Dunn of the Hammes Co., the general contractor for the stadium renovation project.

◄ The Packers commemorated the rededication of Lambeau Field by putting this "Rebirth of a Legend" patch on the players' jerseys for the season opener against the Minnesota Vikings on Sept. 7, 2003.

▼ After a week of celebrating the renovation and rededication of Lambeau Field, the season-opening game proved to be a disappointment for quarterback Brett Favre, left, and the rest of the Packers. The Vikings spoiled the day by beating the Packers 30-25. Next to Favre on the bench are running back Ahman Green (30) and tight end David Martin (87).

▲ Running back Ahman Green heads toward the end zone on one of his two touchdown runs during the season opener against the Vikings. He scored the Packers' first touchdown in the renovated Lambeau Field, doing so on an 8-yard run with 1½ minutes left in the third quarter.

The west side of Lambeau Field at sunset on Sept. 3, 2003, four days before the renovated stadium was rededicated.

Lambeau Field: Green Bay's National Treasure

Publisher: William T. Nusbaum.

Book editors: Jeff Ash and Carol Hunter.

Principal writer: Tom Perry.

Contributing writers: Bob Berghaus, Warren Gerds and Karen Rauen.

Photographers: Holly Balsis, Ken Behrend, Clarence Bredell, Stephanie Bruce, Mike Brunette, Patrick Ferron, Lowell Georgia, Sandee Gerbers, Joan Gutheridge, Paul Ihde, Selena Jabara, Jeff Kriwanek, Russ Kriwanek, Emery Kroening, Steve Levin, William J. Lizdas, Terry McHale, Bob Miller, Andy Nelesen, Mary Annette Pember, Bill Peters, Orvell Peterson, John Robb, John Roemer, Mike Roemer, B.A. Rupert, Evan Siegle, Wayne Trimble, Todd Truttmann and Ken Wesely.

Other photographs: Green Bay Packers archive, Harmann Studios, Neville Public Museum of Brown County and the Henry Lefebvre Collection of the Neville Public Museum of Brown County.

Librarians: Jean Eggert, Florence Hyska, Lynn Komisarek, Diane Robb and Tom Rozwadowski.

Photo scanning and restoration: Blayne Belter, Kathy Colavitti, T.J. Hengler, Jim Hoslet, Jill Kolzow, Scott Olbinski, Tina Tweedale, Bo Yang and Nhu Yang.

Book design: Brad Fenison, Pediment Publishing.

Other contributors: Bob Harlan, John Jones, Lee Remmel, Jeff Blumb, Zak Gilbert, Craig Benzel, Kate Hogan, Mark Schiefelbein and Nick Bandoch, Green Bay Packers; Barbara Janesh, Peter Frank and Mike Vandermause, Green Bay Press-Gazette; Eric Goska, Green Bay Press-Gazette correspondent; James Bartelt, Ken Behrend, Art Daley, Dave Devenport, Russ Kriwanek, Harry Maier and Len Wagner, retired Green Bay Press-Gazette staff members; Marian Maier; Scott Hildebrand, University of Wisconsin-Green Bay, a former Green Bay Press-Gazette staff member; Mary Jane Herber, local history and genealogy librarian, Brown County Library; Louise Pfotenhauer, curator of collections, Neville Public Museum of Brown County; John and Lisa Carpentier, Stadium Sports and Antiques; Marv Niec, Packer City Antiques; and Tom Murphy, Green Bay Packers Hall of Fame.

**Proceeds from the sale of this book
benefit the Newspapers In Education Fund of the Greater Green Bay Community Foundation
and the Green Bay Packers Foundation.**